D1532301

HOPE FOR THE HOME

WAYNE DEHONEY

ALL RIGHTS RESERVED
Copyright © 2001

No part of this book may be reproduced or transmitted in any
form or by any means, electronic or mechanical, including
photocopy, recording, or any information storage and retrieval
system, without prior permission in writing from the copyright
owner.

Cover design by:
Phyllis Fekete

FIRST EDITION, 2001
ISBN 0-9702395-2-1

Printed by
The King's
PRESS
P.O. Box 144
Southaven, MS 38671

PREFACE

A good marriage is not a gift a bride and groom, with sudden delight, discover among the other wedding presents. It is an achievement, a homemade do-it-yourself project. It is built by two hearts and two pairs of hands constantly working at the task over a long period of time.

In this "building project," a tragically high percentage of persons fail because of bad patterns, shoddy materials, poor workmanship, or the lack of adequate assistance and understanding.

The chapters in *Hope For The Home* are refined expansions of sermons delivered in a special series between Mother's Day and Father's Day. During this *family-life emphasis*, we also conducted panel discussions for specified age groups before and after the Sunday evening services. Topics for discussion came from questionnaires, a question box, and directly from the audience. Consultants on the panels included local physicians, gynecologists, family counselors, public school personnel, psychologists, and ministers.

In dealing with family-life problems I feel that churches and ministers desperately need the assistance of these specialists and their knowledge. Much scientific research has been done in this field in recent years. Psychologists, through their depth studies, continue to give us new insights into the human personality so that we are understanding more and more about "why we act as we do." The sociologists, through studies in human relationships, have helped us to determine norms of conduct and attitude. The insights of the marriage counselors, practicing psychologists, and psychiatrists who deal with these problems face-to-face in counseling situations help us greatly in coming to grips with subtle and elusive problems.

These scientists and specialists have aided substantially in defining the problems and their causes. But I believe that the central problems of love, marriage, sex, and marital conflict still demand the full saving power of the Christian answer. Again and again, in all the scientific research, the spiritual significance of marriage

iii

continually breaks through to overshadow the physical and material aspects. In marriage, as in all of life, the Christian ideal prevails as the ultimate in human achievement.

Thus, I believe that God desires only the best for each of his children. A Christian marriage can be one of his means of making that best possible. God, as the giver of all life, has made you what you are, male or female. In this creation, he has placed in you elements of desire and affection that are intended to be sublimely and supremely fulfilled in marriage by your specially created counterpart, a person of the opposite sex. In providing for the full expression of love and sex through this marriage, God imparts to you a portion of his creative power for you to create a character, a sublime relationship, a home, and through procreation a new life. My sincere hope is that this volume will give to you some practical spiritual guidelines to help you achieve this supreme ideal in a Christian marriage.

Wayne Dehoney

FOREWORD

The Sunday Morning sermons which I preached from the pulpit of Walnut Street Baptist Church in Louisville, Kentucky were televised for 18 years and were also mailed out to over 4000 ministers and laity.

It is my pleasure to make them available once again in this collection.

We dedicate them to the glory of God and to the edifying of the church.

ABOUT THE AUTHOR

Dr. Wayne Dehoney is a Minister and a former President of the Southern Baptist Convention. He has been preaching for 62 years and served as a pastor in Tennessee, Alabama and Kentucky.

In 1985, at 66 years of age, Dr. Dehoney retired from the Walnut Street Baptist Church (originally First Baptist) of Louisville, Kentucky.

During his 18 years as pastor, the church built two multistoried retirement homes with 409 individual units, a medical and nursing facility and several educational, recreational and family activity buildings.

With a combination of evangelistic preaching, innovative programing and creative social action, Walnut Street turned around from a declining inner-city church into Kentucky's largest congregation with 6300 members.

After retirement from the pastorate, he became Senior Professor of Preaching and Evangelism at the Southern Baptist Theological Seminary in Louisville, Kentucky.

Dr. Dehoney has been active in the Baptist World Alliance, traveling and preaching throughout the world. He has conducted evangelistic Crusades and organized Church partnerships to Russia, Ukraine, Romania, Kenya, Brazil and China. These missions have involved more than 3000 lay persons and hundreds of other pastors.

Dr. Dehoney is the organizer and conductor of the BibleLand Travel/Seminar that for 30 years has taken pastors and church members to the Holy Land. Under the auspices of Seminaries and Colleges, the tours offer academic credit for students and inspirational Bible Studies for all participants.

A prolific writer, Dr. Dehoney is the author and contributor of fifteen published books. His latest, "The Dragon and the Lamb" published by Broadman Press, is an account of the explosion of Christianity in the Republic of China.

Wayne and Lealice, his wife of more than 55 years, now live at Treyton Oak Towers, 211 W. Oak, Louisville, KY 40203. This is one of the Retirement Centers built on church property during his pastorate at Walnut Street Baptist Church. They have a son and two daughters. Dr. Dehoney has a great interest still in Dehoney Travel, of which his daughter, Kathy Dehoney Evitts, is president. The address is 1024 S. Third St., Louisville, KY 40203. Phone, (502) 583-1080; Fax (502) 583-2351.

CONTENTS

HOMEMADE HAPPINESS

It was on the last Monday in March — a gray day — late in the afternoon — six shots rang out outside the Hilton Hotel in Washington, D. C. — and the president of the United States slumped into a car. An attempted assassination — he was within inches of being killed — the doctors said.

Who was this man that tried to assassinate our president? In the hours that followed, we found out a little about him. John Hinckley was from an upper middle class family — a respectable family. He attended the finest schools. He was not a terrorist — not a criminal — not a thug — no special cause seemed to motivate him. Perhaps, he may have been mentally unbalanced. We do not know.

But, then came the revelation that his family was a very religious family — his mother and father were very active in the church. The news story said he came from a Christian home — and the question is, again and again, how could this happen from someone who was reared in a Christian home?

Now, I am not passing judgment — I do not want to discuss anything about that home — but, simply to say it is a real question: What is a Christian home, anyway?

Many times we see a Christian family behaving in a very unchristian way. He see a Christian family producing anything but what you would call Christian men and women. It is a good question — what is a Christian home?

Well, the immediate answer we give — the easy

answer — is to say: Obviously, a Christian home is a home that is not a Moslem home, of course. Or it means it is not a Buddhist home. It is not an atheist home. It is a home where the people go to church — they have a Bible out on the living room table — they acknowledge there is a God— they live by the Ten Commandments — they are good, decent people.

But — you know — I have known people who measure up by all of those standards and yet, at home — in their home life, they are mean, and they are ugly, and they hurt each other. They are vicious! And sometimes, with all of these formalities of church going and all of the respectability of the community— it is a living hell for those involved in the family — children and parents alike.

WHAT IS A CHRISTIAN HOME?

What is a Christian home? Did you ever think about it? How would you define it? Maybe you cannot exactly define it. Maybe it is something you just feel instead of defining it.

A young man came to the pastor and said, Pastor, I want to be baptized — I am a Christian and I want to join the church. The pastor said, Sit down and tell me about your conversion experience — tell me about your background.

Well, I did not come from a "Christian home" in fact, there was not much of a Christian atmosphere in my home, although my father and mother belonged to a church. They took me as a child but I soon dropped out. I came to college and the only thing I knew — whenever I had a problem, I would freak out on drugs or get drunk. I sort of lived that way.

Then, I met this wonderful girl. She was a Christian. I started going to church with her and I began to discover some things I had missed in life. We decided

2

we were in love and wanted to get married.

So I went one weekend to meet her family. She lived in a little town, and we had to take a bus to get to her home. When we got off the bus, her whole family was there — mother and father, and a couple of her brothers and sisters, several of them were there. And when she got off the bus, they just grabbed her and hugged her and kissed her and acted so glad to see her. And then they greeted me.

I had never seen that in my family. I had never even seen my mother and father hug and kiss in front of us. And I cannot really remember my father ever hugging me or my mother ever kissing me. These folks seemed to be so happy, and it seemed to be so natural.

We went on to the house and went in. They were joking and there was a lot of humor and laughter. Then we sat down at the table to eat. You know, it was like I had seen in the movies — but I had never experienced it before!

Her father said, It is our custom to have prayer at the table — and we always join hands. Would you mind joining hands with us? So we joined hands around the table and he just prayed a simple prayer.

He said, Lord, thank you for this food — thank you for this friend who has come here to visit us and help him that he might grow into a fine young man and achieve all the goals that he has in his heart — thank you for bringing our daughter back to us. He prayed this simple prayer — and when he was through — I just never felt like that — I had never experienced anything like that in my life.

I am now a Christian, and that is the kind of home I want to have. I want it to be full of that kind of joy and relaxed peace and happiness. Now that is a Christian home!

The Bible describes the Christian home in Colossians 3: Paul is writing about some of the characteristics that ought to be in a home. It ought to have kindness and humbleness of mind, and meekness, and longsuffering; forbearing one another, and forgiving one another — put on love and peace, the love of God — and submit yourselves to each other. Do not be rigid, but yield and give to each other. Do not be bitter. Provoke not your children to anger, lest they be discouraged.

Now — how can we put these things together in some practical definition of what makes a home Christian? I have come up with a few words here.

LOVE

First of all, there has to be love. A home is Christian when there is love. Not the Hollywood kind of emotional love — not just the physical sexual aspects of love — but love where there is the real warm acceptance of each other.

That is what love really is — accepting someone as they are — not as we try to make them. If you do not shape up and be like I want you to be, I will not love you. Now, that is the way we try to deal with it — but that is not real love.

A man was talking to another man about his wife and about marriage. Oh, you know, getting married is like buying a phonograph record. When you get a wife, you see what you like — like getting a song. You say, I especially want this song that I like — but you also have to take the flip side along with the song you really like.

And you always have to take the flip side with what you want in a wife. The other man: I guess so — but what do you do when your wife has two flip sides? That says something about the man, not about her.

4

Here is a man saying, I have my mold—I have my patterns — I have my legalism — and if you do not measure up, I am just not going to accept you. You are going to have to change and shape up, because you do not please me; you have two flip sides. Now that is not real love.

Real love is the kind that says, I love you — in spite of the things that are different from me. I can love you as you are. Acceptance.

And that goes for children, too. A child is not afraid to bring home a report card that has a bad grade on it — not because the parent will not do something about that grade —but the child is not afraid that the parent will say, I do not love you if you do not shape up and get straightened out here. Love has to be there.

CARING

I think the second word is *caring.* A Christian home is where there is caring — where you really care about each other. That is a little different than love in that it is the kind of concern that creates the atmosphere in which love can grow.

A woman said to her husband, Why is it you never tell me you love me? You never say that! Why don't you tell me you love me? He finally threw down his newspaper and he said, Now, listen — when I married you, I told you I love you— and if I ever change my mind, I will let you know!

Now — he said he loved her — but — there was not any real care there. There was not an atmosphere in which love could grow and mature. Love is a growing thing. You ought to be more in love as a family with the passing of the days — with the passing of every year. And a family ought to love each other more and more in that kind of atmosphere of caring about each other.

So, love — and caring — and . . .

5

TENDERNESS

And the third word is tenderness. I like that word; it is really the Greek word translated here as *kindness* — kindness is tenderness.

We are shocked by abuse — physical abuse — in our society today. Child abuse. I read this terrible story about the man who took a little child and held it in the hot water until it was scalded and the child died. The child also had a broken bone or two where he had beaten the child. Finally, after the long process in the courts, I read last week where this man was convicted of murder and has been sentenced — and he ought to be! It is a terrible thing — to do that to a little one-year-old child! Child abuse physically.

But, you know, you can abuse a child verbally and it is just as damaging to their character, their self-esteem. I just cringe when I hear some father say rebukingly to his son, What's the matter with you— you're all thumbs — you got two left feet! Can't you ever do anything right? The little fellow just cringes before his father. That is child abuse. Where is tenderness and kindness?

Or there is the mother who says, You are always getting on my nerves — why don't you straighten up — if you don't behave yourself I am not going to let you do this — that — and in anger reflects she is not going to love the little girl if the child does not do what she demands of her. That is not tenderness and kindness.

And then there is the husband who abuses his wife verbally — talking about the old woman, the old bag I married— she is the ugliest thing I ever saw. That is like physical abuse.

Or there is the woman who is emasculating her husband as she abuses him verbally — why aren't you like so-and-so — why don't you get ahead — why don't you

6

make money like so-and-so — why don't you be a man like so-and-so? That is abuse — unkindness.

A Christian home is a place where there is tenderness.

SECURITY

A Christian home is where there is security. That is what marriage is all about. God gave us marriage to fulfill the essential loneliness we have. Christian marriage is to fulfill that loneliness that we have as an individual, so that two against the world can have security. We may lose our job— we may lose the things we have — we may lose our health —and we will lose our beauty— and we will lose our youth.

But we will have each other, and the two of us can face anything the world sends against us. That is security! And the Christian home is based on the premise that we are committing ourselves for a lifetime of fidelity, each to the other in security.

It brings *physical security* — a sense of protectiveness — of protecting each other. The man has a sense of physical protection for the wife; the wife has a sense of protection for her husband. She is going to prop him up; when he is down she is going to lift him up; when he comes in battered by a competitive world of dog-eat-dog — she is there to protect him, to build him back up and restore that ego that has been all but destroyed. There is protection and security there.

There is *emotional security* in marriage and a Christian home. A man said to his wife, If you were a good Christian — if you really believed the Bible — if you would just claim the promises of the Lord, you wouldn't have these periods of depression. Where is your faith? That is a lot of baloney. That is not so!

Our emotions go up and down. Good Christians

7

and bad Christians alike have these waves of depression and elation. We find in the Bible that some of the choice persons of God had periods of depression. Elijah for example, and Paul, and others.

Of course we are going to have periods when we are down — a part of Christian marriage is this emotional security of someone that stands by you and says, in times of your weakness— I will be strong; I will be the one to prop you up. And then, when it goes the other way, you will prop me up — that is emotional security in a Christian home.

And then, *moral security*. That is basic. That is the kind of security that allows the man to say, I have such security in our marriage relationship that I am not afraid for my wife to work down at that office with all those predatory males running around there. She is not going to fall in love with her boss and have an affair down there. I am secure.

Or the wife is able to say, I know when he is off to that business convention at Vegas he is not going to be unfaithful to me. That is the kind of moral security in a Christian home.

Now— do you see what I have said? A Christian home has love, caring, tenderness, security — I have not said anything at all about faith. I have not said anything at all about going to church, being in Sunday School, reading your Bible.

However, these things are a part of it. And, I come to the last word.

FAITH

You can go through a lot of the external forms of religion and not have these things —love, caring, tenderness, security. But you cannot have these things without having a real personal vital faith. Faith in God

8

— an attachment to God's people in the church — personal faith in Jesus Christ that He is Lord. He Savior, and the Lord of your life. Faith is a foundatic stone on which the Christian home is built.

So, I simply ask the question:

Wouldn't you like to have a Christian family, a Chris tian home? You can — if you will make it a priority. Yo say, This is what we want more than anything else — an we will pay the price — the price of priority — puttin; first things first — saying, What shall it profit a man a woman, a couple, if they gain the whole world — yet, they let their family and home become a place of hell or earth? What shall it profit?

This is the greatest thing we can do — above all other attainments in life — to have a Christian home and a Christian family. God, give us Christian homes.

We can start by being a Christian ourselves — and make a personal commitment of ourselves to Jesus Christ.

So, I conclude with this basic of all basics: How is your relationship with Jesus Christ? Would you come to say, I will trust Him as Lord, as Savior?

HOPE FOR THE HOME

CHRISTIAN MARRIAGE

Genesis 2:21-24

Today our world and our society faces many problems. This past week (May '72) President Carter's proposal for gas rationing was turned down by Congress. Whether it was a good plan or bad plan, it still leaves us with a crisis on our hands.

We are facing the problem of the SALT agreement. Is it the right thing or the wrong thing, to make a treaty with Russia? Will we become weak and second class to a communist power bloc in the future, or will we be peacemakers in the world?

Statistics last week reinforced the fact that inflation continues and seems to be getting higher and higher. At the same time, it is predicted that in the last part of this year, or the first part of next year, we will face some kind of recession. And we live under that kind of dark spectre.

But — our real problems today are not financial and economic; those are but symptoms. Our problems are not basically political. *The basic problem is moral.* And if it is a moral problem, *it is a spiritual problem.*

For example, inflation is an economic problem, but the root of the inflation is a moral problem that arises out of the moral decay that is upon us today. Our absorption with material things. We cannot keep spending more than we take in without cheating our children; it is immoral to leave that kind chaos to the next generation. It is immoral for us to operate on the principle that Social Security is constantly bankrupt and we must take today's income to pay for yesterday's commitment. There comes an accounting. Inflation ran rampant in Germany following the war until the day when one loaf of bread cost 10,000 marks! That is immoral. When we cannot control desires and our wants for things, we have economic problems.

The greatest moral problem we are facing — greater even than materialism where we believe things will answer every need — *if* I can just have that house — *if* that car — *if* the swimming pool — *if* I can have what someone else has — my problems will be solved. No — even greater is the *problem of family* — The disintegration of the family.

Some authorities today are asking the question: Can the family survive in this society of ours, western civilization?

There has been a steady breakup of the family. Factors like the Industrial Revolution greatly affected the families that moved from the farm to the city and became lost in the crowd. The Equal Rights Movement, which in itself is right, has brought problems with it — working mothers and working wives. And the effective development of birth control and increased sex outside marriage. All of these things have affected the family.

And so the emerging nations are saying, If this is what is happening in the western world, we do not want you to import the breakup of the family to our societies. A speech at the UN recently said: In the emerging nations, there is a greater emphasis on the family and its importance. And in the western nations — the industrialized nations — there is the disintegration of the family.

Newsweek magazine, *U.S. News & World Report.* *Time* magazine, all within the last year have carried major articles and issues on the family and its breakup. They carried such significant figures as these: First of all, the divorce list in the newspaper is sometimes longer than the marriage license list. They cite such facts as, one of every six children in America today under 18 years of age now lives in a single-parent family. They cite suicides as the second major cause of death among young people 15 to 24 years of age — indicating the emptiness of home life and the lack of stability.

I was talking with a student at Vanderbilt whose roommate committed suicide and he said, You do not see it in the headlines of the paper — but we had seven suicides last year on our campus. It is staggering, the effect that the breakup of the family is having upon young people today!

Then, by age 17, one of every ten girls will have a child. Think of it. Half of them will have a baby out of wedlock. Fifty percent of all young people under the age of 19 say they have had premarital sex.

Now, all of this points to the problem of moral decay within the family and its breakup. And, at the root of the breakup of the family, are the faulty concepts we have of marriage itself. If you do not have the right relationship in marriage between a husband and wife, you cannot have the right atmosphere in the family. If there are tensions and problems in a marriage, then those problems are reflected in the family life.

That is why I want us to talk about *Christian marriage*. I do not want to pile any more guilt on the shoulders of many sincere, honest, loving, wonderful people who have made every effort in the world to have a Christian marriage and it has failed. It was beyond your control — either your own self-control because of the mistakes you have made or the mistakes of the other person — and you have had the death of a marriage; or you are living in a hopeless situation and it seems a Christian marriage is impossible. I do not want to add to your guilt.

At the same time, I think we ought to put up the ideal. This is what we hold up as the desirable achievement for our children for the next generation — we missed it, but maybe they can learn from our tragedy, our heartbreak and our sorrow.

God has a plan and a purpose for marriage. The world has its way; and it is diametrically opposed to God's way. When we go to God's way for marriage we find peace, harmony, joy, fulfillment and a growth of our personhood. But when we go the way of the world — we have gone that way too much — we find the destruction of personhood, of peace, happiness and joy. And marriages fail.

So, this morning, I want to point out five characteristics of Christian marriage. Let's measure ourselves — our ideals — with these five characteristics.

CHRISTIAN MARRIAGE IS DIVINE

You say, Well, that is obvious. No, it is not. Some people think just because they stand before a clergyman who says, I now unite you in holy matrimony, that suddenly something spiritual has happened and they now have a divine marriage. That is not so! There is nothing magic in the words, holy matrimony. And the legitimatizing of your marriage in the church by a minister does not automatically say it is a Christian marriage from henceforth.

A Christian marriage acknowledges that God must make that marriage. God, through Jesus Christ, must be in the two individuals who join together in that ceremony. You cannot have a Christian marriage without two people who are Christians— committed to

14

Christ, to His church, to Christian idealism.

A lot of people today have only two sides to their marriage. They acknowledge the social obligations to society. They send out announcements and say, We are living together here. Then, there is a legal obligation. They must get a marriage license; they must have a legal ceremony and it becomes a contract

But, notice, as a triangle with only two sides is open and it collapses easily. There is nothing to hold up a marriage when it is just social and legal; there is no real support.

That third side is *spiritual*. It is by the power of God that a prop is put between the legal and social dimensions of marriage. God comes into that marriage, that union, and into those lives, to give stability and strength. So — marriage is divine. It has a spiritual dimension. You cannot have a Christian marriage until you acknowledge that your life is planted in Christ and it is your determination as two Christian people to have a Christian marriage.

Then, second. . .

CHRISTIAN MARRIAGE IS TO BE PUBLIC

It is not to be done in secret, in the dark. I counseled with a young couple who said they were secretly married. Our parents would object — we are in school — we would have problems if we announced our marriage. I said, You are not married. Oh, yes, we are. On our knees before God, we committed ourselves to each other — we are both Christians — we are both faithful to each other. All we need later on is the legal aspect of this. That is not Christian marriage.

Christian marriage has a strategy in it. You gather together the public that is close to the couple — those who love and care for both of them. In the presence of

15

the company assembled, the minister says: Will you take this women to be your lawful wedded wife, to love and to cherish, forsaking all others, clinging only unto her, so long as you both shall live — do you so promise — not just to God — not just to each other — do you promise these who love and care for you — this public assembled here?

Why is that so important? The natural result of marriage is children. When a child comes into the world somebody has to feed and care for that child, give that child a home, and educate and prepare that child for mature responsibility in society. This couple stands before those who care about them and says, We are ready to accept publicly this responsibility. We pledge and promise to you we will take this responsibility. Christian marriage involves a commitment to a public out here as well as to God.

Then . . .

CHRISTIAN MARRIAGE IS COMMITMENT

It is not a contract — like a contract to buy a car or a house. This is how we break up if it does not work out. It is not a contract — it is a commitment — a permanent covenant. It is for a lifetime.

That is the Christian ideal — that is what God wants and purposes for everyone. And the word, "if," is not in Christian marriage. "If" you stay beautiful — "if" you provide well for me — "if" we do not have any hard times —"If" we still stay in love —"If"— no! It is a commitment— a permanent commitment.

That rules out two things that are popular today. It rules out *trial marriages*. There are those today who say it , it's good— let them try it out. What he needs — what she needs — is to get married. Needs a husband — needs a wife —that will solve their problems. Marriage is not going to solve a single personal problem

16

you have. Hear me now! I will talk more about this later. Marriage will intensify the personal problems you have instead of solving them. Trial marriage does not work.

And second, it rules out living together without even a trial marriage. That is popular. There are folks shacked up all over the country. I could not even say that ten years ago. But it is so common — you read it in the paper — you talk about it. A son in college — is shacked up with a girl — they are just living together. What will we do? When he comes home he wants to bring that girl home. And they write Ann Landers. What will I do? That is ruled out in Christian marriage. The unique thing is this— there are those who argue and say, This is the way to try it out and see if we are really made for each other. Isn't it a whole lot better to try this for a little while? That is better than getting married and then need a divorce later.

The statistics say: Those who do try it — whether they marry the one they tried it out with or someone else — the divorce rate is twice as high! Instead of being good for them, it is really bad! How can that be?

A psychologist said this is the problem. They move in together and try it out. One say's, I can split — I don't have any obligation — no ink on a piece of paper that ties me here.

That means any hour one of them can split and go somewhere else. It means both of them are always on guard. They cannot be themselves — they cannot really get to know each other honestly and openly. They are afraid to be honest with the other. Only when you have a lifetime commitment to each other can you really get to be honest and be yourself.

In this commitment, know that you can bare your greatest weaknesses to the other and find strength and help and you can grow together. That is the genius

17

of Christian marriage — it is commitment for life.

So— it is divine — it is open, public — it is commitment — it is covenant — and then . . .

CHRISTIAN MARRIAGE IS FIDELITY

A commitment to fidelity. That simply means, chastity, an old-fashioned word that means *purity*. Be faithful. You do not commit yourself to love each other from henceforth; there may be times when love grows cold. Love is an emotion that flourishes and dips. Sometimes you look across that table and wonder, How in the world could I love that thing sitting there?

She did not say. I promise I will love you from now on. She said. I promise I will be *faithful* to you — I will be true to you. And Christian marriage is built on this principle of fidelity and chastity.

When you make that kind of commitment. It means you have thrown away your parachute. You are in it for the rest of your life. Hold up that ideal.

You have read about Lee Marvin and the trial. This girl lived with him six years and one of them decided to split. She sued him for some contractual money she said he owed her; and the judge gave her $100,000 for rehabilitation. A good thing I was not the judge; I would have given her $6 million not because she deserved it by what she did. And I would not call it rehabilitation; I would call it an educational fund. Here is a way to say to all these folks. You just cannot move in and live together without accepting some responsibility for it. Financial responsibility and moral responsibility. Responsibility to society — responsibility to law. It is time we as Christians stood up and said, This is the ideal; we will not settle for less than that. Then —

18

CHRISTIAN MARRIAGE IS A PROCESS

We read a moment ago: Therefore shall a man leave his father and his mother, and shall cleave to his wife; and they shall be one flesh. What does that mean?

It does not mean a fleshly physical union, the sex experience, one flesh. It is not inherent in the text. It is not inherent in Christian teachings. When two people come together physically, they do not become one flesh.

One flesh is the growing process of two individuals — two separate personalities — so committed to each other in love and fidelity and trust— they grow together until they become as one. Two identities, but one heartbeat — one goal, one purpose in life. It is not automatically achieved at the snap of a finger when a minister says, I now pronounce you husband and wife. You are not one flesh like that instantaneously. That ceremony here at the front of the church that sends you out is not a key to a lovely garden— where you will live in beauty and wonder the rest of your life — that is not it.

This ceremony sends you on a pathway to a vacant lot. And you are given the tools by which you can build a Christian marriage— by a lot of hard work— a lot of commitment — a lot of love — a lot of forgiveness— a lot of understanding.

I close with this. John Wood, pastor of First Baptist Church, Paducah, and I were fishing on Kentucky Lake several years ago. We were talking about what we preached on last Sunday. He said, I'm working on a sermon on marriage. Let me ask you — is love and marriage an artesian well that just flows up — I saw you — the minute I saw you I fell in love with you— and it just bubbles out and just swells up in you? I said, That is the romantic ideal. And he said, I have come to the conclusion that marriage is a pump with a short handle; you

19

have to work at it all the time.

And he is right. Marriage is a work that requires the best you have. It is the highest achievement outside your relationship with God through Jesus Christ. Christian marriage and a Christian home, I think, is the highest achievement two people can achieve together in life.

God grant that you will make the start on it. It is not too late — whoever you are—whatever position you are in — you can go out today and say, I am going to be a Christian. You can say, I am going to live by Christian principles. I am going to get my ideals up there — this is what I will aim for. And, regardless of where you are, you can make a start today.

CHRISTIAN MARRIAGE

PART II

Genesis 2:21-24

On this Mother's Day I want to talk about Christian Marriages. I want to talk about a Christian home. I want to talk about a *family*. I want us to think together: What makes a Christian? What makes a home Christian? And I would like to start by telling of something that happened in my life a number of years ago.

Our family was on vacation in north Florida during a hurricane. They did not have the forecasting system as they have now; we were not alerted to the seriousness of the storm, and we slept right through it. We heard on the radio the next morning that a severe hurricane had come very close to us.

As we drove along that north Florida coast we saw the devastation that had been wrought by the waves and the wind. Boats were turned upside down and thrown up on the beach. The docks had been torn apart. And then we saw the beach cottages that had stood on stilts and pillars — they had literally been torn apart, as from an explosion, and cast way back into the mangrove swamps.

Yet, in all this wreckage of the storm, again and again, we saw this house standing — that house and that house — that building seemingly untouched by the storm. As you looked more closely, you could see a difference. Those that had withstood the waves and the wind were

Vol. XIII   May 13, 1982   No. 19

anchored fast on a solid foundation.

I think it is a parable on marriage today — on family life — on society itself. For today, the hurricane winds of change are sweeping all about us. And, in these winds of change there is destruction galore. The waves of immorality and change seem to attack every stable institution we have. Everything is being shaken. Business structures — the school systems — the church life— and, above all, the family life and marriage are greatly shaken and many are destroyed by these storms of change.

Now I could start by giving you the bad news: The problems we have in marriages today. The gross immorality in our society. Surveys telling us how many college students are sleeping together, and saying, We never intend to get married. Marriages that are failing and unhappy— the divorce rate. We know the bad news. The storm has hit; here is destruction all around us.

But the good news is: There are families that are standing —homes that are secure — marriages that are happy and solid, and permanent — and that is where we need to focus. Christian marriage is alive and well today. If we have any kind of hope for tomorrow in this world, in this society, we need to recognize solid, sound marriages and build on them. That is the building block and foundation stone of all orderly society. Everything else rests upon the solidarity and security of marriage and the family.

So —let us talk about Christian marriage:

The first question I need to ask is: What makes a marriage Christian? How would you define a Christian marriage? Not all marriages are Christian marriages. Some so-called Christian marriages do not make it.

What would you define as the basic elements in a

Christian marriage? I think we would have to start by saying.

I. A DIVINE MARRIAGE

A Christian marriage is a *divine marriage*. By that I mean, it has in it a belief and trust and faith and confidence that God is in that marriage. It is not just a physical relationship. It is not just a human earthly relationship. There has to come into that relationship a kind of spiritual power; it has a seal of divine approval upon it.

Now — we recognize that marriage has many sides to it; marriage has one very real side out here called the *physical* side of marriage. That is a very real element of marriage.

We know from the most primitive animals to the highest of man, there is a biological clock that begins to work from the time of birth. The time comes when that clock develops some urges, drives, impulses, instincts, for the purpose of reproduction. There is an attraction of opposites, male and female. They came together and breed and produce. This is a part of God's eternal purpose for the perpetuation of life on earth. We need to recognize that here is a *God-given, God-planned, God-ordained, God-purposed* drive in all of life; and it exists in human beings to come together, male and female, so they can reproduce.

The only problem with that: Those who take such a naturalistic and humanistic approach to mankind say that is all there is to it. Man is just a higher animal; these instincts are no different than the instincts of dogs and cats.

There is a phrase in common usage today that bothers me— seems so degrading to my humanity, to my spiritual instincts. It is a terrible phrase: sexually active. You have seen it. A mother writes to Ann Landers:

23

My daughter is just 14 years old and she has become sexually active. What shall I do? Shall I give her birth control pills or not? Ann Landers answers: Yes, since she has become sexually active, you had better do something to prevent her from getting in trouble and having a baby.

That is the way we talk about alley cats getting sexually active and we lock them up. We begin to look at human beings as though they are animals, and we try to stop these problems on a physical animalistic basis. Jane Randall, the anthropologist who has done some excellent animal documentaries, used the term sexually active. And we talk about human beings!

But there is more to marriage than this urge to find a mate. That is one side of a life and God has a way for us to fulfill that drive — that instinct — within a certain legitimate framework. It is indiscriminate with animals. But God planted in man something different that causes him to discriminate, causes him to say this is more than a biological experience. It must be guided and directed and channeled in a moral and responsible way. That is one side of marriage — the physical.

Another side of marriage, is *legal* and *social*. Early in history, mankind said if this drive was not channeled properly, it will hurt people, and human personality is of great value. The children would have no father if this was indiscriminately practiced, as animals practice it. Human beings have to be nurtured by a father and a mother. Then, property becomes involved. So, mankind very early put restrictions on the physical side of marriage. It must be socially and legally controlled.

So — today — we have laws that say here is the way you legalize this physical experience. Marriage under certain conditions, and you stay married with certain obligations.

Now— the greater portion of society today sees

24

marriage only in terms of these two sides. If I open up that triangle, you see two sides. It does not make a whole—it is a physical experience and a legal experience. Therefore they say. Physically I am attracted — legally, let's get a legal marriage — and that makes marriage! THAT DOES NOT MAKE MARRIAGE! That does not close the triangle.

And that is our problem. That is why we have the loose attitude prevalent today. I say the following not judgmentally; I say it with great concern. An actress has just divorced a fifth husband, and the writers commenting about this famous person say. What is she going to do? There is nobody else for her to marry— nobody of high enough standing. She will have to recycle her former husbands; and they are speculating which one she will take. Physical attraction and then legalize and that is it! Is that all there is to marriage? No!

The Christian understanding and interpretation of marriage says there is a third side: A *spiritual side* that says God intended from the beginning to be in it, to be a part of it. Two people say there is some thing and some power outside ourselves, beyond ourselves, that comes into this relationship. We believe it is God who puts His seal, His approval upon this marriage.

There are a lot of marriages today where people are physically married and legally married. But they are not Christian marriages because God is not in the marriage. God has to be in the people that are in the marriage. There has to be faith and belief in God — some feeling that God is with us and we have His approval, His seal on this marriage. We, as a people, believe this. We do not always practice it — but deep down, we believe it is God who seals the marriage, who comes if we let Him and seek Him.

I will show you how that works. At Pineville, Kentucky, the church and the pastorium were just two blocks from the courthouse. As they came out of the hollows from the mining camps to get a license to get married, they would be looking for a preacher. And they were told, A Baptist preacher lives just two blocks up the street.

One day this fellow came, I want to see about getting married. When and where? Right now — Who to? — she is out in the car — bring her in. She doesn't want to come in — she is timid — you got to come out and see her. I went out to the car; she was blushing and embarrassed. She had come to get married — but she did not want to come to the church.

I said, Why do you want me to marry you? I want a preacher to marry me — I don't want no Justice of the Peace to marry me. I want to be really married —I want a preacher to marry me. Why? It is holy matrimony, ain't it? A pretty good answer. So we went inside the church and had the ceremony.

What was the girl saying? I want to be really married — and marriage is more than just living together and getting a certificate from the government saying it is legal. God needs to be in it, too.

So — I must start out by driving down this stake: Christian marriage is *divine* in origin — it is *spiritual* in its foundation.

The second thing I could say.

II. A COMMITMENT

Christian marriage is a commitment, not just a contract. A marriage has contractual agreements, contractual responsibilities, of course. But it is more than a contract. It involves the person committing themselves to certain things.

First of all, it is a *commitment to priority.* Jesus said, *For this cause shall a man and a woman leave*

26

father and mother; and cleave to each other. All other human relationships are secondary to this relationship established in marriage.

That says a lot to us. It means we need to cut some apron strings. The girl who has to run home to mother every time something goes wrong — or the boy who cannot stand on his own feet and has to keep going back to mother — comparing his wife to his mother — needs to cut the apron strings.

Marriage is the basic relationship, physically and materially, in life. Only one other relationship is likened unto it and that is with God. For this cause shall we leave all other relationships and cleave to each other.

It also means a different kind of commitment about other claims on our lives, whether business claims, professional claims, recreational claims. These are really secondary claims upon this basic commitment to marriage. Man and wife together need to evaluate the other claims and prioritize them in their places.

It is also a *commitment to fidelity.* I need to say that, because a lot of people think marriage is a commitment just to love. The ceremony says. Do you promise to love and cherish henceforth forever? The problem is that we interpret *only love* as the basis. It is difficult to make a commitment where love is level and continuous all the time. Love is an emotion that goes up and down, up and down.

I often say to young couples, You love each other, don't you — but one of these days one of you is going to stomp your foot and say, I hate you — and really mean it. You really will hate them it that moment, at that time! Love is a mixture of hatred and love. Love grows and develops and wavers, up and down — back and forth.

But *fidelity* is something else. Fidelity means I will

be true to you. I will be so mad at you sometimes I could wring your neck and kill you, but I will be true to you. As we learn to adjust and live with each other, we have our conflicts. I love you more sometimes than I do others because I know that is human nature. Emotions ebb and flow. I do love you. But, above all, my commitment is, that even when you are unlovable, or I am unlovable, you need not worry — I will be true to you.

And that is the ultimate security of marriage. That is the Christian concept needed in this world today. That is what gives stability and security and trust in marriage.

I have said marriage is divine in origin, it is a commitment and it is . . .

III. A MYSTICAL PROCESS

Christian marriage is a mystical process. Jesus said, And the two shall become one flesh. That is a mystical process — that two lives can become one flesh. Think about that.

In my ethics class at seminary we discussed this a long time, and the prevalent idea among the students was that this meant the two become physically one flesh in an act. Our professor said, No — you missed it. The two shall become one flesh; they shall come together in a growing and growing togetherness until the day will come that they will be as one, so inseparable that you can never get them apart again.

They go to the cafeteria and order the same kind of food. She takes carrot salad — I take carrot salad after 35 years. That is our first choice. She says, I will get that pie and split it with you, because we are both going to get the same kind of pie. We eat the same things. Some say you even look alike after you have been together 35 years.

The point is — this mystical oneness comes because you have the same goals — the same purposes. You are drawn together in the same conflicts, the same troubles. We have a beautiful ceremony in a wedding here. Between two burning candles is an unlit candle, the unity candle. The bride and groom each take a burning candle and together, they light the unity candle; and the two are one in a single flame that can never be separated. The Indians used to say once two streams flow together into the river they can never be separated.

You build a marriage, first, by saying it is spiritual in its foundation — God is in it. Then secondly, it is a commitment. And third, it is a mystical union where two become one flesh; so after 35 years or more married to Lealice Dehoney, I cannot conceive of life without her; it is such a oneness that I cannot even think any other way. Jesus said, That is what God desires for every one. Many miss it because of human frailties, sinfulness, or mistakes we make.

But, the glorious truth is that our God is the God always of power, of strength, of another chance. And He comes in His grace, His love, His mercy to say you can overcome whatever obstacles you have — if you have had a marriage that failed — if you have a marriage that is on the rocks — if you let immorality creep into your life in a way that you cannot get hold of yourself — regardless of what the mountain is — the grace and power of God can help you conquer it.

Let me close with this story. In 1924 the first assault was made on Mt. Everest, the highest mountain in the world; Hillary was the Englishman who took the group. They climbed 24,000 feet up the side of the mountain, made a base camp, and he and a partner tried to assault the summit. They died up there and they are still buried amid the avalanche snows of Mt. Everest.

Coming back to England, one of the party was lecturing. With slides he was telling others about this great conquest of Everest and of difficulties along the route. He brought the slide show to a close by very dramatically turning to the picture of Mt. Everest on the screen, and talking to the balcony: Everest! We tried to conquer you once, but we were not able. We assaulted you the second time, but you defeated us.

Then, looking at the mountain he said, But, Everest, I want to tell you, we will conquer you, because you cannot get any bigger, but we can! And, of course, we did get bigger, and in other expeditions they conquered Everest again and again — because there is within the human spirit and human life the capacity to get bigger.

By the grace and power of God, you can be bigger than you are right now. The mountains of trouble and adversity, the difficulties, the failures, the defeats of yesterday in any area, whether it is in your marriage or your personal life — those mountains cannot get any bigger, but you can! By the grace and power of God, you can!

With faith in God, with trust in Jesus Christ as Lord and Savior, you can overcome whatever mountain you face today. I have talked about marriage — but whatever that mountain is — if it is a habit, a problem, a sin, or doubt — whatever it is — let the grace and power of God come into your heart through faith in Jesus Christ — now — today! You can be bigger than anything you face — you can overcome it!

REDEEMING MARRIAGE
IN A SENSUAL WORLD

Genesis 2:18-24

Marriage needs redemption just as we as individuals need to be redeemed by the grace of God. You cannot have the ideal in marriage unless the grace of God has touched that marriage, redeemed it and changed it. Marriages fail because people fail; people fail because they are sinners; and we are not redeemed by the grace of God sufficiently to conquer the problems of life.

Now, I struggled with this message. I confess I come with a great anxiety as to how to present it. I do not want to come out negatively; that will help no one. I do not want to come out with a sense of guilt and failure. I want to say there is hope — there is promise — there is light at the end of a tunnel — there is a way out — there is a great ideal: It lies before me. By the power and grace of God, I can achieve it in this matter of Christian marriage.

What *is the problem*? It is acutely focused for us by the Census Bureau report that came out in March 1977 on the changes in the life-style in America. Here are some of the statistics.

It says a million and a half people are living together outside marriage — tolerated and largely accepted by secular society as a way of life. That compares to 654,000 in 1970 — three times as many today!

The divorce rate continues to rise. Of every six family units with one parent — five are women. In other words, in five of six cases — the woman in divorce, in separation or desertion, keeps the children and has to care for them. That is a changing pattern — a real problem — a crisis situation, sociologically. Young people are getting older before they marry — an increase in the median age of a year and a half, both men and women.

What has caused some of these changes? First of all, the change in attitude toward marriage itself — even this generation. Let's look at marriage as a social institution.

Until recent years marriage was *an economic necessity* for both the man and the woman. This was true in Biblical days. It was true in the frontier days of America. It was an economic arrangement, for each had something to give the other. They needed each other. We have the stories about the women taken westward to be wives for there were no women in the West. They would gather women in the East who wanted a new life, a chance to be somebody and to marry. They came from all walks of life, even prostitutes, but here was a chance to get respectability. They brought them out, matched them up, and they were married.

Why? The man had to have clothes and food and someone to care for his children. So she wove the cloth, she sewed the clothes, made the garden, set the table, nurtured the children. The man, in turn, gave the woman respectability, security and protection. He gave her a livelihood because there was no way a woman could make a living unless she had a man to look after her.

That pattern existed until the industrial age changed it. In our affluent society today marriage is not the only option a woman has. She is educated. She has equal rights in employment. She can make as much money as a man. She does not have to marry for security. The man can buy his clothes tailor-made. He can get his TV dinners. And he likes his independence. He does not have to depend on a woman.

The sociologists are saying marriage is no longer an economic necessity for either the man or the woman which makes marriage stand on its own. It must stand on the basis of the relationship and interpersonal relationships of the two. As a result, a woman married to a cranky, brutal, alcoholic husband no longer says, I do not have any other choice. She says, I can leave him — get a job— I do not have to put up with this. And she should not have to.

In the same way, the man does not have to live with a surly wife that is cross, bitter and hostile. He says, I will leave you — I make enough money— I can support you and another woman.

Another factor that enters in — *roles are changing.* The woman has become equal with a man in rights and privileges before the law and in employment. Marriage today is a kind of partnership. It is not unusual for both man and wife to work and share equally in making the money. They share equally in the home responsibilities. He helps do those things at home that, formerly, the woman did alone. But she is working with him and their joint income produces this better life for them.

Some of the conflict we have in marriage today is the blurring of these roles. We think in terms of yesterday and rural life — the woman's place is at home. The man's place is making the money. When they change these roles, they have problems, psychologically, adjusting to them.

It is easy to decry these statistics. But not everything is bad. Now hear me properly when I say this. Maybe we are to the place where we can more nearly achieve what ought to be the ideal Christian marriage. People today are marrying for higher ideals than just a housekeeper and a breadwinner. They are marrying to find personal satisfaction, emotional security, fulfillment and support. The goals are more intangible, but they are more spiritual. People are saying, I expect a marriage that does more than just put food on the table and clothes on my back and a place to live. I want marriage to be an enriching experience for the two partners and for the household.

So my contention is a positive one. What a day for a church to say, This is exactly what God wants you to have in marriage. He wants it to be a great spiritual experience — to be enriching and fulfilling — to be the kind of partnership that enhances your personality and makes a fuller person of you. That is what the church ought to be doing.

I think we ought to be doing it in three areas. First of all, we ought *to be holding up this ideal for young people looking toward marriage.* Secondly, we ought to *help those who have failed* in this the greatest enterprise of life. You missed the mark before —but, listen, there is an ideal and, by the grace and power of God, you can do it.

The statistics tell us that four of every five people that are divorced remarry. We cannot shut our eyes to that reality. We had better say to these who have been divorced, We have something to help you make the next one go. Build on a Christian foundation. That is the reality of life around us, and that is the approach this church has tried to take in a Singles ministry. We have a place and a message for you.

Third, we ought *to say to those who are already married,* you can make your marriage better. I could be a better husband — sure I could. Even if I am happily

34

married, it could be still happier. We ought to make a contribution there.

We read the Creation story of how woman was made of man. I want us to see what Jesus had to say. In Matthew 19 we read: *For this cause shall a man leave father and mother, and shall cleave — the man shall cleave to his wife — and they shall be one flesh.* Wherefore they are no more twain, or two, but one flesh. What therefore God hath joined together, let no man put asunder.

The key word: *What God hath joined together.* That is the foundation on which we stand. Jesus said they become a partnership. What kind of a partnership does Jesus say it will be?

A DIVINE PARTNERSHIP

Marriage is sanctioned by God and God is involved in the true marriage. I would picture marriage and its dimensions in terms of an equilateral triangle.

The first side is *the physical side.* There is no denial this is one dimension. Marriage relates to sex and the physical; that is one of the beauties and glories and wonders of it. There are those who say that is all there is to it. But there is more to it than that.

Secondly, it is *a legal relationship.* Society has laws and regulations that govern it. That is why I have to be licensed to marry people. It is not enough just to be an ordained minister, I have to be posted with a bond at the courthouse. Society says we must keep order here. There are rights, privileges, property, children, responsibilities. So laws are made to restrict and control marriage and the circumstances of it, the age of marriage to protect children. Some would say that is all there is to marriage — physical — legal.

But Jesus said the foundation is this third side. It

35

is divine. It *is a spiritual relationship*. And the triangle is not complete until you get the spiritual base there.

What is our problem? Too many people live on a physical and legal plane only. They have a marriage with just two sides. How can you talk about God being in a union, even though a minister marries them, when their lives are not in God? They are not Christians! They do not care about God. It is the problem of the human heart, the problem with sin, the problem of commitment with God. So we cannot even talk about marriage and the concept of Jesus Christ and the ideal He sets for us unless we say the foundation must be spiritual—in God. You must be in Christ and, together, you want to have a relationship blessed by God and sealed by God.

Now, notice, when you put divine restrictions and controls on marriage, this rules out a lot of things. It rules out open marriage. This rules out living together. This rules out contractual marriage.

A SUPREME PARTNERSHIP

For this cause shall a man leave his father and mother — the woman leave her father and mother — and the two shall cleave together and be one. It is the supreme relationship in all human affairs. A greater tie than the tie to your parents. Who is to come first? There is no question about it. In the marriage that partner must come first. We have a problem with loyalties here. Children come and the mother says the children must be the priority. No. Even children are second priority to this relationship.

The experts say there are three crisis periods in any marriage. There is *the first year,* the peak crisis. If they can make it through the first year, they will get along through six or seven years. They are cutting the apron strings. The first year is a test as to whether

36

they can make the break and stand on their own and have their own identity in marriage.

If they get past that, *the second peak* usually *comes when they get two children.* Then comes the struggle as the mother, worried and exhausted, commits herself to the children. The man gets absorbed in his business.

The *third period comes in the empty nest* when the children are all gone. Here are two people that have been married for twenty years. Suddenly they look at each other and they are strangers. They have not grown together in their interests.

This is why Jesus said it is the supreme relationship. You have to put it above everything else in life. That is the ideal so you can pass these crisis periods and make it.

A MYSTERIOUS PARTNERSHIP

It is truly *one flesh.* This is not a physical reference. Many would say the actual physical mechanical act in marriage is what makes one flesh. That is not so. That is not inherent in the text, or in sound theology. That is not inherent in practice. If that were so, it would mean that God would say the first act of sex in adultery, or fornication, or anything else, would legally and in God's sight make those two people married. No, that is not so.

One flesh is the broad concept of two people becoming one in every dimension of life. In goals, purposes, dreams and heartbeat. The glory and wonder that as the Indians used to say. Two streams flow into one river and can never be separated again. It is the beauty as when we have two candles burning here with an unlit candle in the middle. Following the wedding ceremony each takes a burning candle and, together,

37

they light the third candle and blow out the other two. So, it is one flame burning from now on. A mysterious union that God joins together. When God enters into it, it becomes divine and supreme.

How do we achieve it? I have jotted down ten commandments. Maybe these are practical and will help you.

The first commandment. Throw away your parachute when you marry. Do not say, if it does not work, I can bail out. Don't leave a back-door open. Enter it saying. This is my commitment to fidelity — I am going to stay with it. If you cannot enter into a marriage with that kind of commitment, you are not ready to get married.

Second: *Establish a definite link with the church.* Do not cut yourself off from a source of spiritual supply. Cut an apple branch from the tree and the apples will wither. Even if you are a Christian, cut your life from Christian fellowship and the fruits of your marriage will wither. How often, after a couple marries, they are so excited and enamored with each other they cannot get up on Sunday morning. They drop out of church and you do not see them until they have about two children. Then they get worried about those children and they come back. Now they already have problems. Establish yourself in the church from the start.

Third: *Look for the right models.* What kind of couples are you associated with? Those whose marriages are in trouble? No. Get some friends who have strong marriages. Form associations with them. This means you are going to have to cut off some people. If we stay around these folks, the first thing you know we are going to think it is the norm to have problems and be separated. Find some Christian couples that are succeeding in their marriages.

Fourth: *Communicate.* Be open and honest. Do not

38

let the sun go down on your wrath. Do not let your hard feelings and hurts carry over to the next day. Be able to say, Forgive me. Let's wipe the slate clean and start new tomorrow.

Fifth: *Determine to grow.* You do not stop growing when you get married. Do not quit reading and exercising your mind. Learn some new things. Get some projects. It is tragic to see a man outgrow a woman. She does nothing and he grows because his career demands it. Soon they are so far apart, they have problems.

Sixth: *Develop a wise healthy attitude toward sex.* What God hath made clean, let no man make unclean. God has established a sacred relationship that is to be performed inside the marriage relationship. Yet outside it, it creates guilt, social problems. Inside marriage, it is to be the finest expression of love and affection. Master it in the framework of marriage.

Seventh: *Learn each other's needs and try to fill them.* We all need love; we need to be told we are loved. We can give love, but we need to receive love too. Giving love is never complete until we get it back. It is not enough to say, I feed you — I give you my paycheck — isn't that a sign I love you? Of course not. You need to say, I love you.

Isn't it enough that I fix this meal for you and work my fingers to the bone keeping this house up? No. Tell me how much you love me — how proud you are of me when I come in beaten and worn down from my job.

Eighth: *Avoid tyranny and selfishness.* We all want to dominate someone else, yet no one else wants to be a doormat. A man taking a political survey asked the woman, What party does our husband belong to? She said, You're looking at it. Do not dominate. Arguments start over nothing and, before they are over, they end up with one trying to be supreme over the other, I am

39

right, you are wrong.

Ninth: *If your marriage is in trouble, get help.* Do not hesitate. Go to Christian friends — others who have good marriages and say, How did you work through this? Go to professional counseling. Finally, go to God when you need him.

Tenth: *Keep on grappling with your problems.* Do not give up.

Keep struggling with it. Don't give up and you will have a marriage that will endure.

GOD'S PLAN FOR YOUR FAMILY

Use your imagination — picture a mountain top from which there descends a narrow twisting winding road— a dangerous road with many obstacles — many precipices without guardrails — great embankments — on the other side a twisting hazardous road that leads down to a broad happy valley below.

Then, would you imagine — at the top of this mountain you see a line of automobiles and people getting in the automobiles two by two, a man and a woman. They start driving down this treacherous road, dodging the obstacles, skirting the curves and the embankments. Sometimes one hand is on the wheel. Then the other, and sometimes both of them are on the wheel.

Then, can you imagine this awesome terrible statistic — of every three cars that start down that road, one of them will wreck — shattered and completely destroyed. And the occupants, two, maybe passengers they picked up along the way, are broken and crippled. What a frightening prospect!

That is the picture of marriage today. This is the road of marriage, treacherous, filled with obstacles, dangerous curves. And here in an automobile of marriage, a man and a woman, sometimes they pick up children along the way — there comes the tragic wreck of marriage before they reach the happy valley when they would be secure — where all is well. The tragic wreck of marriage which we call divorce.

In the United States today we have the highest divorce rate of any country in the world. For the first time in our history (1976) both the President of the

United States and the Vice President, our models of leadership, are married to divorced women; and the latter himself is a divorcee.

A CRISIS

Now, what is happening? The breakdown of marriage in our culture and our society — which foretells the shattering of family life — and both the historians and the sociologists call it the crisis in Western *civilization*. Only twice have we seen total disintegration of the family. Once, 300 B.C., Greek civilization; second, in Rome about 300 A.D., they tell us. Both times the complete disintegration of the family was followed by the fall of the nation and the culture itself. So, the authorities are saying this is what lies ahead unless this trend can be reversed. They point out the same symptoms, the same factors today as in Rome and ancient Greece. The focus in the family is on things as more valuable than the persons involved. They point out parental irresponsibility for children — the child's rebellion against parental authority — juvenile delinquency which is always preceded by adult delinquency. Then it is all summed up by the disintegration of the whole concept of marriage.

Already today we have proposals to substitute for marriage. Contract marriage says we will try it awhile and then quit if it does not work. Or living together without even the sanctions of marriage, trial marriage.

Now— the question facing us —

WHAT IS THE CHURCH'S RESPONSIBILITY?

What shall be the reactions of Christians? How are we going to deal with this? Can we bury our head in the sand saying we have no voice, no word to speak on the crisis that faces the American family and our society? What is the church's responsibility?

THE DIVORCED

Here we have the wreck of marriage — statistics — millions of people whose lives have been broken. A man, a woman, some children — crippled, scarred— they are suffering; they are wounded as they started on the journey in life's greatest and most exciting experience. They never reached the valley below. What shall we do about divorce?

A popular approach: Count the statistics — there they are — another and another — then throw up your hands in holy horror and say, What a terrible tragedy! We can decry the statistics and the situation — but, is that enough?

Another approach is *judgment.* Passing judgment on those who have wrecked their marriage. Those who successfully navigate the treacherous road say — and this is so typical of us as Christians and as a church — we point a finger and say, You are unrighteous; you have done wrong; you have sinned! You are divorced; you are a moral leper! I can't touch you. We shut our hearts and our doors, we don't care what has happened to you; it's wrong!

I had a pastor friend who took a rigid stand on this matter. He said, I'll have nothing to do with a person who is divorced. They cannot sing in our choir; they cannot teach in our Sunday School. He was literally saying they are second rate members of the church. If they come, they are to sit in their shame and be quiet; they cannot have any part; life has ended for then as far as God is concerned. He was horrified to think that anyone would even ask him to marry someone who had been divorced.

But, I saw the tragedy when his own 16-year-old daughter as a Junior in high school ran off and married a 16-year-old boy. These two children had a child, and then two years later she came home with a child. I saw

43

the guilt and agony he went through when he realized you are not dealing with statistics; you are dealing with people who have been hurt. What do you do for them — how can you help them?

I started my ministry saying God had called me to touch people and help them. If there is anything in the Christian faith that I am sure of, it is the love of Jesus Christ, of the forgiveness of God, and His acceptance of those who come asking forgiveness. I want to proclaim that love; I want to help the wounded along the way.

This is what our church tried to do. For example, in the seminar on divorce on Sunday nights we looked at the biblical teachings — what is the ideal —what is God's purpose for your life— how do you pick up — where do you go from here now that you have missed the highest ideal and target?

Our church is here to show love, understanding, kindness to those that have been wounded. Not like the priest and the Levite, Jesus said, left the beaten man for dead. They passed on the other side, he is unclean. But Jesus said there was a good Samaritan who reached out his hand and touched him, picked him up and loved him. I want people to talk about our church as the church of the Good Samaritan — concerned about people, touching and helping.

But, it is not enough to say we are going along this road and pick up the wreckage and minister to the hurt and wounded. The church must do more than that. Then we . . .

MUST WORK ON THE ROAD

There are a lot of obstacles to marriage that wreck them, and society has put them there. The church should have a strong and consistent voice. We must stand against those things that destroy marriages. We need to throw off the rocks — false concepts and ideas of romantic love that we see on television. Alcoholism is an enemy of marriage. The false idea that if it does not work out in a few months, just separate and start over again. We need to say this is not the right standard. We need to hold up to the world the right standards. Clean the highway of obstacles and make it safer.

But, we need to do more — as a church we should—

PREPARE THE DRIVERS

Train them before they start on this journey. That is why we have a youth program, youth camps, sessions for young people to say, Before you start out on this adventure of marriage, let us help you prepare for it. It is a treacherous road; there are traps; society is telling you lies about sex. If you go in this direction and engage in immorality, you are sowing seeds that can destroy your marriage later on. Let's take our stand as a church. Then—

STRENGTHEN MARRIAGE AND FAMILY LIFE

Let's help the marriages that are already on the road and having a hard time. We have family life conferences. And I am preaching on it. I am going to talk about building blocks for a Christian marriage. Is your marriage going to be triumph or tragedy?

GOD'S PLAN

Now, I talk about the Christian family and God's plan for every family. The Bible gives us a very clear plan.

This Bible gives God's ideal plan for marriage. The ideal is one man for one woman joined together in one union for life. A glorious, beautiful ideal. Like a mountain spring that starts on this hillside. Far on another hillside completely unknown to this one, another mountain spring starts and flows down until at last those springs come together and the waters mix and inter-mingle; the two streams become a river never to be separated again, to flow in an ever-broadening river down, down into the valley, getting broader and deeper with the passing of the years.

That is God's ideal. The two shall become *one flesh,* not just a physical relationship; it is the blending together of lives and purposes and goals, of two into one like the streams. That is what God wants for you — the ideal.

What is *God's ideal for a child? That every child shall have a good mother and a good father.* Anything less than that is less than what God wants and a child deserves. And where there is just one parent with the children, there is often the great risk of crippling and scarring, of sending into the world a child not equipped and ready to handle life.

What is God's purpose for the family itself? The church was modeled after the family. It is one of fellowship and equality; not an arrogant dictatorial father where everyone jumps at his word — not a selfish self-centered woman where everyone bows to her wishes; not arrogant children who are rebellious against parents; and the parents cower in fear, tyrannized by their children. God's ideal for the family is to have an equality of love and sharing one with another, each in their place.

I heard a story: Professor Little held a little position in a little college in a little town. And he drew a little salary and lived in a little cottage and had six little Littles at home. Somebody said, Professor Little, you're in a little college in the little village living in this little house on this little salary with six little Littles to care for — how in the world do you get by? He simply said, Every Little helps a little. That is God's purpose for a family — all sharing together.

46

But, someone says, I missed the ideal. Yes, many have. We missed the ideal on number one, or number two, or number three or all three. What shall we do about it? The gospel of Jesus Christ is always the gospel of beginning again. If you have missed, it does not mean that you cannot start again and do something now.

God has a plan for every life; how we should live, the kind of character, the kind of attitude, how we should relate as Christians in this world. He spells out His plan in the Sermon on the Mount: He talks about peacemakers and turning the other cheek, purging the heart of malice, bitterness, if we have anything against someone else. And he sums it up with this almost impossible ideal. Be ye therefore *perfect*, even as your heavenly father is perfect!

How many of us are perfect? I fall far short; we all do —what do you do? Quit living? Give up? No— God forgives me and God's power and love help me work toward this ideal.

I want to suggest to you five wonderful keys, or secrets, to find God's plan for your family and your life.

SECRETS OF FULFILLMENT

First, you must decide to do something about it. You cannot say it will work out or it won't work out. You must make a commitment to God — you as a Christian, maybe your partner will help you, or you may have to do it by yourself — but you say you are going to work on it. I am going to do something about our family life.

This I believe — any person who is a genuine, sincere, seeking, open, growing Christian with this determination can inject life into a family situation and improve it immensely. Decide!

You may think your partner and your family are

47

not interested in this — you will be amazed at their response. The wife of a young pastor, in despair, felt lonely and left out. My husband is going his way in the church. The counselor asked if she had told her husband about this. No. Try it. A few days later she called. I talked with him and found he was hurting too. I learned he needed me and I needed him. That is a start. You decide.

Secondly, together, sit down and decide what values are important *in your marriage.* What are the real values? We get so distorted in our values. I know fathers who spend hours night after night taking a boy to Little League ball games to see him excel in athletics. But that same father resents his son or the mother asking him for 15 minutes to help the boy with his math homework. That is distortion of values!

Decide the spiritual values. Is God really important in your life? If you really believe in God, how can your children know? How do you demonstrate it at home? What are you going to do about Sunday? A businessman said. I've been tempted to get a lake cottage — but I don't dare do it. I would promise myself and my family we would go down on Friday night and come back Saturday night to attend church. But I've seen my friends — before you know it they are there every weekend — life is as secular on Sunday as during the week. I don't dare do that. This was a wise man; he had his values right. The spiritual life of his family was most important.

Then, third, decide what means you will use to preserve these values in your home. What habits and practices — One practice is the family altar. You say, I've tried that. The picture of yesterday's rural America does not fit today. All the family around the table or the fireside; father reads the Bible and prays. They did not have an automobile, no television. Robert Burns portrays this picture in "Cotter's Saturday Night" so beautifully.

48

But you say we can't do that; in this society today, there may be a half dozen families in all Louisville that have an evening with the family altogether. How can you do it today?

I was with a family for the evening meal where the father read from a devotional magazine with scripture; he asked for special concerns for prayer. They joined hands, and I with them, around the table and prayed. A simple grace, but the power of it! A demonstration of the values that are important. Falling on that child's formative mind, day by day.

So, decide on the mechanics, the things you will do. What about books? What kind of records for the stereo? A man comes home to a wife who has been listening to gospel hymns and was humming "What a friend we have in Jesus" and threw her arms around his neck when he came in. He might come home a little differently if he found you in that kind of spirit. What kind of atmosphere?

The fourth: Reach outside your home and get some help. You cannot do it by yourself. Attach yourself to a church; be active and involved in it. A church that meets your family's need, where you can serve. Have the right attitude toward it so your children can see by your example that you love the Lord, and the church, and you are serving in a Christian spirit. How important that is! A man said, I did wrong; I was bitter, critical; I said mean and hurtful things about my church — I have changed now — but my boy is grown, and he is hard and indifferent. Pastor, I want you and the church to do something. I could not be unkind enough to say. What can we do? You have cast the mold.

Be active in that church. Be right in your relationships. Support it. Give. Go. Work. It is important.

Finally, the last key: *Attach your family to other families that set the right model* and example for you in a Christian family. All of us draw around us three or four or so families and we find all our relationships in these families largely.

Where do you make your friends? Business? Social-club? Country-club? Or in a church, and a Sunday School class, a small, age-group class where you find other Christian families. My family can see other families that are stable and Christian.

That is why our church tries to have a seven-day-a-week program. It is not enough just to preach on Sunday morning. The activities building, multiple activities, all kinds of programs, recreation, social life — all center in the church.

That is God's plan for your family. I challenge you — if God be God, serve Him. If Christ is savior, give your life to Him. If the Bible is the word of God, then study it and lead your children to study it in a systematic way. If the church is important, belong to it and work in it!

If your marriage and your family is a sacred institution, then build it on a spiritual foundation by committing your life to Jesus Christ as lord and savior!

There is a glorious promise in Proverbs 12:7 — *The house of the righteous shall stand.*

Will you claim that?

A FATHER'S LAMENT!

II Samuel 18:32

If you mix a cake and it does not turn out right, you can just throw it out and mix up a new batter. If you are writing a poem, you can scratch out the words if it does not sound right; and if it does not look good, you just tear up the paper and throw it away and start again. If you are laying a brick wall and you finish it and see that it is tilted, you can knock it down and rebuild it. If you are constructing a house and you discover you have made a mistake, you just tear it out and redo it.

But not so with a life. You cannot just say, I have made a mess of it; I will just clean the slate and start over again. That is the life that you are shaping in your children. Above the doors of the YMCA are these words: What shall it profit a man, if he gain the whole world and lose his own son? You see. You do not get a second chance on that. That is what is called life's irrecoverable loss. Some things you can lose in life and still recover. Lose a fortune and make it again— but lose a son, and you do not get a second chance.

I want to talk about a father's lament. The cry of a father who was a great success in life as a king, but a total failure as a father, he felt; and we see the agony of his heart as he cries out.

This passage is the story of David. Civil war is in the land, and the leader of that insurrection is his very own beloved son, his favorite son of his favorite wife. Absalom is out not only to take away from him the kingdom, but to take his very life; he wants to kill his father.

David has been driven from the capital city and from his throne. With his loyalist troops he has retreated into the safety of a walled city in the wild country across the Jordan. As the troops line up that morning and march in review, the scriptures say, by the hundreds and thousands, he divides them into three armies. And he gives his charge to each commander: Go — fight the battle — win for the kingdom — save the kingdom — save the throne. But be kind to my son, Absalom. Don't let anything happen to him, even though he is the leader of the enemy army. And the battle rages, and thousands are killed.

At last, a messenger comes running, and we read this account as David is waiting. Cushi says, Rejoice, 0 king, the victory is ours — the enemies have been dispersed — we have won the battle. And David says, What of my son Absalom? What of him? And, unable to say the words — He is dead — hanging in a tree by his hair shot through with arrows — cut down and thrown into a ditch covered with stones — soldiers coming by to spit upon him — unable to tell that gruesome story Cushi says, They that are against thee and Absalom are alike. In other words, they are all dead.

With those words, the king is now the father. He drops his head and begins to weep as he climbs the lonely steps into the tower. Those below him hear him as he cries out his lament, Absalom, my son, my son Absalom! Would God I had died in your place. The cry of a father who has been a great success in life. He had achieved everything that a man could want to achieve. From humble beginnings as a shepherd boy, he rose to the very heights to be king of all Israel. Under his leadership—a successful administration — he consolidated the warring tribes, unified the nation, brought economic prosperity to the land, built a magnificent palace, had peace with the neighbors, organized many structures within the kingdom that made it a benevolent and good administration.

In fact, it became the golden era of Israel and in the years and centuries to come, the Israelites and the Jewish people would point back to the glories of the kingdom at the time of David the greatest king. More than that, he was called a man after God's own heart. A man who was sinful and wicked — yes— but a man who was so spiritually sensitive that he wrote those beautiful verses we know as the Psalms that have become, literally, the hymnbook of the Christian faith through the centuries. This man, such a glorious success as a king, has seen the failure of a father. And when he looks at this irreplaceable, irrecoverable loss of a son he says, I would give my life to take your place.

It reminds me of Calvin Coolidge, President of the United States through two successful administrations. When urged by his friends to run the third time in 1928, he simply said in one of the shortest declarations of political intent ever recorded: I choose not to run. No other comment, no other statement. In his memoirs, he told of the tragic untimely death of his only son and he said, When my son died, it took all of the glory out of the presidency. Think of it — a broken-hearted father — President of the United States. But he said, There is no glory in it because my heart is broken out of sorrow for my son who died.

I want to talk about this irrecoverable loss that we can suffer. And I want to recognize in the very beginning that it is not easy to be a father and fulfill the responsibilities of fatherhood in the complex society in which we live with all the external pressures that are upon us.

Dad is sort of a minority stockholder today in this business of child rearing — no question about it. The baby comes and mother has the responsibility. In most young families, Dad is working so hard to make a living and get ahead. It is a tough job. The first six years he does not see much of that little baby as it grows into a child to send to kindergarten and to school. You turn that child over for six hours or more a day — sending them to a school you can no longer choose — under a teacher with whom you have no choice — teaching a curriculum about which the public has very little to say — with classmates and influences over which you have no control. So you have lost a large stake in the environment and control of your child right there.

That child comes home from school and turns on the television set for an average of six hours a day in the American home. Then there starts the bombardment of all kinds of influences that change their values, their attitudes, and create desires and wants in their lives to buy and to be and to do. These things are totally different sometimes to your ideals and purposes for them. So they move through life and one day you wake up and discover you have had very little stake in their lives and very little to do in their lives— and then only to discover it is too late. So, I want to talk to you about fatherhood and parenthood and the responsibilities. I want to talk about what God expects us to do as parents in the family. I think of some very simple statements. Maybe you can remember them and stake some of your practices in life on these statements.

The first statement I want to make is: *Dad, keep yourself in the picture.* Keep yourself in that family picture. So many forces are working to take you out of the picture — keep yourself in it. That statement comes from a story I share with you from Nathan Porter, presently a pastor in Arkansas. His former job had him traveling all over the country visiting campuses to recruit missionaries for the Home Mission Board, so he was away from home all the time.

One evening at home his little girl crawled up in

his lap to show him what she had done in school. These are pictures I drew in art class. One was a flower, another was scenery. Then he asked about one that had some people drawn in it. That is the family. The teacher said to draw a picture of your family. So he looked — there was a woman — that was mother. Here was a little girl — that was her sister. Here was a little boy — that was her brother. Here was another little child and she said, That's me. That is all there were — just four. A picture of the family. He said, Where is your daddy? Oh, she said, I forgot — I forgot. And he said it just cut his heart out when she said that. She forgot to put daddy in the picture — because daddy was never in the picture. Whenever they talked among the family, he was not there. And he said he wept.

The next morning he went in to see Dr. Rutledge and said, I have got to change my schedule, if not my job! And he told him what had happened. I have to get back in the picture — I have been neglecting my children and my family and I cannot keep on doing that — I am not going to do it. He rearranged his schedule, and one day she came home with a picture and said, Look, daddy, the teacher had us draw a picture of the family again and I have you in it this time. Now that is a simple little story that I hope you will not ever forget. It is just to say, Keep yourself in the picture.

There are some men who are home all the time. But they do not get in the picture. They do not care about their children. There are others who have to be gone a good part of the time, but they make it count when they are there and they stay in the picture they make sure they are in the picture. That is the first thing. Dad, keep yourself in the picture.

Then the second thing: *Give yourself to your children.* What do they want from *you?* They want you! And that is the way you keep yourself in the picture. It is not the things you buy them, but the things you do

55

with them in giving yourself to them.

Dr. Kenneth Chafin tells of this experience with his daughter, Nancy, when she was about five or six years old. She crawled into his lap one evening. When he asked, What do you want, she said, I just want to be with you and talk to you — are you going to be home tonight? He said, No, Nancy, I have to go back to the seminary. Oh, I thought maybe you would be here tonight for a change. I wish I could. But I have a commitment to go there. Oh, I wish you could be here with me. Well, Nancy, I do not have those kind of choices — I have to speak to some students, husbands and wives, about how to be good parents. Then it dawned on him — here he was going over to talk to them about how to be good parents and his little girl was sitting in his lap saying, Daddy, I want some more of your time — you do not have time for me. So he said, I tell you what, Nancy, I would like for you to help me tell those parents what they ought to do. What do you think is a good daddy? What does a good daddy do? Help me with my speech.

So Nancy said, A good daddy knows how to catch a butterfly. He remembered — they got a jar and made a net and caught some butterflies together last summer. A good daddy knows how to start a fire. He remembered — just last week in the cool of the Fall evening, Barbara had said to start a fire and he had asked Nancy to help him build the fire. He helped her lay the kindling and strike the match— that is a good daddy.

A good daddy can fly a kite. He remembered. A good daddy can catch a fish. He had taken her fishing — a little pond — they caught a couple of tiny bream but she thought they were the biggest fish in the world.

That night as he went to his engagement, he pulled out the list. He thought about the profound things he was going to say about psychological analysis and parents today and communication and how you can do it — and all the things you would do. And he looked at the list — right there it is! That is how to be a good parent! On this whole list there was not a single thing that you could buy. The child was not asking for you to buy a single thing! She was saying all you need to do is give yourself. That is the greatest thing you can give your child! That is why I say, Give yourself!

A third thing I would say: *Set the right example.* Be conscious of the awesome responsibility we have to set the right path — to walk the right way — because our children are going to model after us. They are going to have a marriage about like the marriage we set for them in our example. They are going to treat their spouse about the way we treat our spouse. They are going to actually deal with their children about the same way we dealt with them. We are modeling for them all the time. They are going to have an attitude toward life much like the attitude we set ourselves.

I remember the story of Clay Doss who was president of the old Nash-Kelvinator Corporation. He told this story about his nine-year-old son. The little fellow wanted his daddy to go with him downtown to buy some little gadgets at a magic shop. They shopped around and got about ten different items and brought them to the counter. The girl was very discourteous, she did not wait on the customers and the line of people backed up and it took them thirty minutes to get waited on. Finally, the girl took the items and rung them up and gave them back in a sack. As they left the store the boy said to his daddy, We sure did get even with her, didn't we, Daddy? Being so impolite to us. What do you mean? Didn't you notice — she did not charge us for all we bought. She only charged us for one thing instead of ten — we sure got even with her. The father said, No, son, she was impolite to us, but that is dishonest. We owe her some money. She does not deserve it — it was her mistake — let her pay. No, son, that will not do— that is dishonest and we cannot be dishonest. We have to take the money back. But she does not deserve it. When they got home, his dad said, In the morning you are going to take that money back because that is being dishonest — and we are going to pay for what we got.

The boy rode the streetcar back and took the money. He came back and told his dad, I told you so— she did not even appreciate it — she was not even nice about it. She did not even thank me for it. I told you so. We shouldn't have done it. No, son, that was dishonest. And he thought the matter was closed.

A couple of months later, however, his wife said, I will tell you what your boy told me tonight. You know, he usually crawls up in my lap and hugs me and we talk a little and he lays his head on my shoulder. Tonight he just laid his head there and said, Mom, I think I have the most honestest daddy in the whole world. I said, What do you mean? — Then he told me the story of what you said and how you said you have to be honest. Clay Doss said, I have received honors galore, even medals in military service, and titles; but I would rather have that one compliment from my son than all the medals I have ever received when he said in his stumbling English. I have the most honestest father in all the world! Set the right example!

And then, fourth, *Give your child a worthy inheritance.* Leave them something that is worthy. We like to leave them a good education; and any parent that is worth his or her salt ought to be concerned about a child getting the best education possible. You ought to work to get it for them. You would like to leave them some financial security; you like to see them have it a little easier than you have; although it is because it has been hard that you have been able to do it. Sometimes we try to say no pain and, as a result, there is no gain.

We would like to leave them a wonderful environment where they can enjoy the beautiful clean rivers and pure hillsides and the game and fish like we have had it. We are concerned about the environment — we would like to leave them a good environment. And we would like to leave them a political system where there is freedom and opportunity like we have enjoyed. Freedom from tyranny.

But, you know, I believe I could live with something less than what I desire on every one of these points if I could be sure I could leave them one thing — that is a great, vital, personal faith in God. I think it would absolutely destroy me today if I were to believe that my grandchildren one day would turn their back on what I believe about God, about the church and Jesus Christ and what my religion means to me. If the religion ran out in my family with the next generation, I think it would break my heart. For my grandchildren to look at their old granddaddy saying, That old broken-down preacher — I just don't believe any of those old superstitions he preached about God, and the ridiculous things he used to say about the Bible, and the foolish allegiance he had to the church — we just don't believe any of those things — I think that would break my heart. I think I could accept my children not having some of the freedoms that we have today — if they could have the power to live under oppression. If they had the faith I know, I could accept their not having the things of life that have made it rich for me. I think they could still have a rich life without a lot of things, if they had the faith I have.

What I am trying to say to you — dad, mother — you cannot give your children something you do not have. But you ought to leave a worthy inheritance, and that worthy inheritance is the kind of faith you have that you share with them. The kind of relationship you have with the Lord Jesus — the kind of relationship you have with the church — that is what counts. Leave them that.

How can we do this? Only one way. We are imperfect fathers and mothers; it is hard for us to do everything right. We are going to do a lot of things wrong. But we can ask God to help us do it. Where we fail, God comes in with His grace and mercy. He helps us and He helps our children to see us as human beings — faltering and failing and stumbling. But we come to God and confess our sins and they see us before God— see us praying and practicing our faith and asking God to help. In so doing, we can bring it out all right — we can make it go.

Sing "Room at the Cross." That is the simple statement of it. There is room at the cross for you and for me — for a dad that is having a hard time being a father— for a parent that is having a hard time getting it all together — for an individual who is saying, I have slipped away and I just realized that I have to get back to the basics. Nothing is more fundamental than my relationship to the Lord and the relationship to this church and to Christian people.

And when we come to the cross and, on our knees before God, we say, I am here, Lord, renewed, rededicated, giving my life to You — then it gets our lives straightened out in the right order.

DADDIES AND DOLLARS

II Samuel 18:33

And as David reviews his troops and sends them out against the armies of Absalom, he waits in the towered city for the report of the end of the battle. And the report comes back— The armies of the rebels have been defeated and Cushi, the messenger says, O king, even as all your enemies, so is your son.

The king has won. The father has lost. We read the father's lament in vs. 33: And the king was much moved, and went up to the chamber over the gate, and wept: And as he went, Thus he said, O my son Absalom, my son, my son Absalom! Would to God I had died for thee. O Absalom, my son, my son! Life's irretrievable loss — for a father to lose his children — not necessarily physically, but to lose them.

Look at the theater marquees. Look at the advertisements on the entertainment page of the paper. The number of X-rated movies, the number of R-rated movies. Look at the reviews; at the end it says, Glimpses of total feminine nudity, profanity abundant in the film, four letter words — but a good film, you ought to see it! A good story!

Somehow we are led to believe that adultery and extramarital affairs, sex before marriage, drugs, alcoholism, abuse and sexual deviations are just patterns of normal life — and that every family has this and every life should have it. Everything comes out all right just the same.

Look on the newsstands. What is printed and sold

today? Do you realize that the magazine business is no longer a subscription business? Most of the magazines sold today are delivered by truck to newsstands, to drugstores, on the street corners.

Why? Because they cannot be sent through the mail! Pornographic material is against the law. But it is sold openly for your boys and girls and mine to browse and buy as they please.

Look at television. Right into our homes. And the trend in the industry. I was interested this week, and shocked, with a story. Don Dorsey of the Courier-Journal, TV and radio critic, announced that ABC this next fall will replace Mary Hartman, Mary Hartman with a new sex movie. Now, they say that Mary Hartman is going to look like Goldilocks when this comes out.

He tells the pattern of the story: Jessicate Tate will be a Gracie Allen type mother sleeping with a 28-year-old tennis instructor. A 14-year-old daughter and little son watch all of this. Corinne is a nymphomaniac teenage daughter. The father, Chester, is a skirt chaser and there are his exploits with other women. The story of the lesbian and homosexual are in this. The only straight person in the whole story is going to be the black butler. Everybody else is going to be abnormal and deviant in some way, and this is going to be at prime viewing time for the American public to look at and say, That's the way life is! Laugh at it and accept it as the way of life.

We can look at the front pages of last week's papers and see the direct result right here in our own community. They announce that one out of every five births in Jefferson County this last year was to unwed mothers. Three times as many as 15 years ago. This in spite of the openness on abortion and the openness of birth control facilities for anybody at any age. Three times as many — one out of every five births to an

62

unwed mother!

And child pornography is right here at our doorstep. With the arrests right here in this community, in the Old Louisville area and the west end area — arrests of those engaged in juvenile, illicit, perverted sex — where they cataloged at least 30 juvenile boys engaged in male prostitution. Right here!

Something is happening to us. Everybody is standing aside and wringing their hands and saying, What's the matter with us? Where are we going? Down the road to Sodom and Gomorrah as fast as we can go as a society? As a western civilization, as a nation, as a community — where are we going?

There are many experts trying to put a finger on the problem — and I am no scholar or expert in this field. But I hear what they are saying; and there is one thing they agree on.

Most of them agree that the first thing that has happened has been the deterioration of the family unit, the breakdown of the old-time concepts of one man and one woman for life, fidelity in marriage, and the stability of the home. It is gone, they say.

Then they move a step further: There has been the loss of the father in the family. In the breakup of the family there has been the vanishing father. He has disappeared from the scene.

Maureen Green, who is a *Time* editor and feature writer for several other magazines, in her book, *Fathering*, deals with this whole thing and traces it all back to the problem of the loss of the father. She has for the subject of one chapter. "The Vanishing Father."

She says he has disappeared in two ways: He has disappeared physically from the scene so that one out of every five homes in America today does not have a father in the home for one reason or another — divorce, desertion or death. Six million children are being

63

reared today in the families of America without a father. He has disappeared emotionally as a father. The father as the father of the household is gone!

Let me just talk in a very practical pointed way about the responsibilities of a father and how all of this hinges together with our Christian faith.

FATHER'S NEGLECT

Somehow, we as men in this society, and as fathers, have gotten our minds focused on the wrong goals to where we think the end in life is a material physical success. Just as David.

David was a great success as a king. He could have written a book that would have sold millions of copies today on *How I Made It From Shepherdboy to King!* Or *How I Made A Million Dollars in Politics.* He was a great military leader, he brought together the warring tribes and brought Israel into its Golden Era. He was a success as an author and writer; he wrote the Psalms that stand today as a monument for us. His name is still on the lips of millions of people 2900 years after he died.

He was a success in every way except as a father. When he measured all these other successes he wrung his hands and said, 0, I would give all of these up if I could have been a good father. Absalom, Absalom, my son Absalom, would I had died for you!

We have the same kind of twisted values when we get focused on the wrong objectives as men and as fathers today.

I will tell you a strange thing that happened during the offertory. I was thinking about my message, and I got up and preached. As I left the service, I walked with Hazel Rushing and something went through my mind— Hazel Rushing — she was to sing. I said, Hazel, are you going to sing in the next service? She said, No

I just sang. What? I don't even remember it. I was sitting right there. She looked at me and I knew she was crushed. She said, I thought you were praying for me. You were looking right at me.

You know what had happened — I was thinking, what is my introduction — what am I going to say — how do I get started into my sermon — my mind was so totally focused on that one thing that I could not even remember she sang. I didn't even know she was standing here singing. Now that is the kind of trick our minds play on us when we become focused on certain objectives. We can blank out and block out everything else.

I say that to say— this is what happens to us too many times as fathers. We get focused on this job — on our promotion — on our career. We get focused on making money — and we absolutely blot out our family, our children, our relationships to then. And it is just as real as that thing that happened to me a few moments ago — just as real. We are not even conscious they exist.

What happens? We suddenly discover one day that we have been substituting dollars for daddies and it does not pay off. The day comes when a boy or girl says, Yes, you gave me everything in the world I could want except the one thing I needed — that was you and some of your time. A father's neglect.

FATHER'S ROLE

In her book, Maureen Green says this is a real problem in our society today. The role of the man. The *role* of the father.

I spoke in McAlester, Okla., some years ago in a revival at the First Baptist Church, and I also spoke at the penitentiary. As I had lunch with the warden who was a deacon in the church. I said. You know the thing that struck me about that group? They were so young!

65

You could have put suits on them and I would have thought I was at a college commencement service. How does this happen?

He answered. This is becoming more so every day. The prison psychologist spoke up. It is the weakening of the male image in our society. It is a loss of the father image. As a boy grows up, from 5-12 years old he is very impressionable. This is the time that establishes his pattern of thought and conduct as he relates to authority, to the rights of others and to property rights. If he does not have a strong father figure to tie to, either in a physical father or a substitute father, a strong schoolteacher or scoutmaster, friend, uncle, a father figure — he grows up twisted and warped emotionally. He does not know how to relate to authority. That is when he winds up in prison.

In the decade since that revival, I have seen the increasing problems that have come from the weakening of the role of the father. I am aware of the ERA— Equal Rights Amendment, and the feminist movement. I think women should be treated as equals in rights. I want to treat my wife that way. I want others to treat her that way.

But I am not talking about rights — I am talking about *role.* There is a difference. God made us different as men and women. He made a woman to be a mother in the role of a mother, and made a man to be a father in the role of a father, and these two role are important in the family relationship. It is important that a girl should have the right kind of mother to relate to emotionally. It is important that the boy should have the right kind of father to relate to emotionally.

And when these two lose their roles and identities and they become alike — the woman goes into the world to say. I am going to be a man in a man's world, a competitor with him — I am going to be masculine in the way I deal — I am going to cuss like he does, drink like he does — I have just as much right as a man to do everything a man does— and man becomes sort of the errand boy for the woman at the house — when the roles become one. Then you have the problem of the girl. She does not know whether to relate to her daddy or her mother for an image. And the boy does not know whether to relate to the daddy or the mother. This is where you get the emotional mix-ups.

The situation in Miami. Fla., with Anita Bryant over the homosexual laws — I do not know a lot about that — but this much psychologists tell me: There is something happening in the identification process, and it is happening because fathers are not fathers to boys, and they get the wrong identity; they grow up twisted and all mixed up.

They need our love and our compassion and our concern because they have been made that way by somebody who failed to do what they ought to do in life.

FATHER'S EXAMPLE

I am concerned about the future. I would like to give my children the best heritage possible. I am worried about ecological problems we face. I wonder if my children will be able to swim in the streams of this country, or will they be polluted. I am wondering if my grandson or granddaughter might be able to walk in the woods and see animals. They may be all gone.

I am wondering whether we are going to have clean air to breathe. I would like to give them the heritage of a clean environment. I am worried about the economic future. I wonder if we are going to be so debt-ridden, and I wonder as the shift of money goes to the Middle East, what lies ahead for our whole economic system? And the capitalistic system that has made us what we are today? I worry about that. I would like to leave my children as good a life as I have had, if not better.

I would like to leave my children the same kind of freedom that I enjoy under democracy. They may be living under a Socialist or communist government two generations from now.

I would like to leave all these heritages to them. But, you know, I could accept the idea that they might have to live under an oppressive government — they might have to live with less of the good things of life — they might have to live in polluted environments — I could accept that possibility — if I knew that I could leave them a religious and spiritual heritage, a faith in God, and the personal presence of Jesus Christ in their lives in such a way that they could live under those adverse circumstances and be victorious. It would break my heart more than anything else to think that I left them a better environment, more affluence, greater freedom and an economic system as I have known— and yet they did not get from me the heritage of faith in Jesus Christ!

Nothing would destroy my soul and spirit any more than to see myself an old wrinkled granddad, and my grandchildren, teenagers or young people, pointing to me in a rocking chair and saying, Well, there's the old man. He's got a lot of nutty ideas about religion. Yeah, he believes in the Bible. He believes in God. He believes in the church. He has some old-fashioned ideas about sex and marriage and this sort of thing. He is peculiar because we don't believe any of those things.

That possibility would depress me more than anything else in the future. For, above all, I want to leave my children the heritage of my Christian faith.

And, Dad, that is what it is all about. Nothing can take the place of you as a Christian father. Nothing can take the place of you as a Christian man in this world.

I don't want to add to the guilt of some today who

68

are beset by circumstances they cannot control. You lost a daddy, there is not a man in your family structure. But, I want to say, that puts a greater burden on the rest of us in the life of a church, in the fellowship in the family of God because, within the family of God there ought to be some substitute daddies — in Sunday School teachers — in a deacon — in a Christian neighbor — in a friend.

That is what all this Singles program is about for single parent families — to say that here in the life of the church there is some reinforcement— there is some way to help in this great test to raise our boys and girls to be Christian men and women in whom the future of this society rests.

Will you respond today?

HOPE FOR THE HOME

FATHER'S PLACE

II Sam. 18:24-25, 31-33

The following is the testimony of Mr. Carl Nussbaum, Jr., in the announcement of his $500,000 gift for the construction of the CLARA NUSSBAUM CHILDREN'S BUILDING:

Twenty-five years ago at the age of 55, my wife advised me to go into business for myself. I had about $6,000 saved at that time, and I always listened to her advice through 58 years of marriage. Another thing she told me: You will have to do better than tithe; you will have to give 20%, 30%, or more. Then she always told me to place God first in all my dealings.

Well, to my great surprise, my business prospered beyond all imagination and all expectation. The more I would give to the Lord's work, the more I would make. And what pleases me most is that this building is the biggest business deal the Lord and I have ever made in my life. It is ten times larger than any negotiation that I have ever made in business. You have heard me say what we do for ourselves alone will die with us; but what we do for God in the world remains and is immortal.

God has given us this time and age in which we live; we have no choice about it. Yet we have a responsibility as to what we do with our time and talents while living in this age. Children are the most blessed assets this world has; God has given them to us to teach and help to grow spiritually as well as physically. Building this Children's Building is our responsibility now. It is the most challenging purpose of this church. No investment we have ever made will bring greater dividends of lasting satisfaction than the molding and leading of the children in the ways of our Lord. It will be for the future leaders of our church, our city and our country.

Friends, I share this gift with you, for today and for future generations of the children of our church and our city. It is my deepest persuasion that when we place God first in our lives, everything else falls in a beautiful and prosperous order. The house is blessed, the business is blessed, our leisure time is blessed; most of all, the children are blessed when we place God first.

Mrs. Nussbaum was a spiritual mother to multitudes of children through 52 years of faithful service as the leader of the same Primary Sunday School Department meeting in the same room at Walnut Street Baptist Church. She went to be with the Lord on March 3, 1981.

MESSAGE BY DR. DEHONEY

I have a preacher friend who moved to a pastorate in Atlanta from East Tennessee. He had two boys, an eight-year-old and a fourteen-year-old. The fourteen-year-old had a paper route in partnership with an older boy. The older boy had one of these modern foreign sports cars and as he drove the younger boy sat on the back of that car and rolled the papers and threw them into the yards, put them in the boxes, or threw them onto the porches, according to how the customers wanted them.

Some of the customers did not like their papers in the yard or on the porch. They wanted them placed inside the screen door. One customer was a retired colonel who wanted his paper inside the screen door every time. But that colonel had two Dalmatian dogs, and they did not like paper boys.

It was always a contest — a war of wits — as the boy tried to deposit the paper and get away from those dogs. They would ease the car up the street very quietly— not gunning it or anything, Then they would stop a couple of houses down and the boy would slip off the car and hide behind the tree trunks until he got to the last clear open space — look around — and then make a mad dash — up the steps — onto the porch — inside the screen door — put the paper there — the instant that screen door squeaked, the dogs came around the house — and it was a mad dash back to the car, jump on the back-end and roar off. He had escaped!

He would come home telling his dad and mother all about these Dalmatians; the eight-year-old brother listened wide-eyed. He did not quite understand about these Dalmatian dogs — but they were something horrible and fierce.

One day after school, the younger boy came in with his friend, Joe. Both were red-faced, puffing and out of breath. We were coming down the street by the colonel's and those damnations almost got us!

THE DOGS OF DAMNATION

Well, the dogs of damnation are after our boys and girls in this world today. They are after their daddies and mothers, too. I could spend the rest of the time delineating how the dogs of damnation are pursuing us and capturing us.

Take the television screen. The violence — the immorality we see coming into our homes. This last week we had a series of articles on the effect of the violence our children see on the screen, movie and television. This is imbedding in them at the earliest age to be aggressive — to hurt — to harm the other person— to beat on

73

people — and to do it without remorse and without conscience.

At the same time, we see the breakdown of all our traditional morality — the breakdown of family life — the sanctity of marriage. Almost every story you see on the screen today centers around infidelity, premarital sex, and/or living together. There does not seem to be any normal pattern of traditional morality portrayed to us as being attractive today.

Or we could shift to the area of drugs. Alan Sears, who is now an assistant prosecuting attorney for the Department of Justice, told how they are zeroing in on the biggest problem we have today in law enforcement — the drug traffic — and Kentucky is one of the major producing areas in the United States — and, perhaps, the largest in the production of marijuana involving multiple millions upon millions of dollars. This is a distribution center for heroin. They already have young men in court — still in their early twenties — who have made $6 million, $8 million, $10 million on illicit drugs. It is capturing us, and the market is not only in the high school — but even in grammar school. The dogs of damnation are all around us!

THE PROBLEM

What is the problem here? What has happened to our society? Andy Holt, president of the University of Tennessee for many years, speaking to a PTA on parental responsibility put it this way: I do not know anything about psychology — I know a little bit about sociology — but I think I can sum up what I believe is the problem. I think the problem is daddies and dollars. Too many daddies are trying to substitute dollars for daddies. Thinking that the one way to make it in life is to make a lot of money — build a business — give your family everything you can materially. That is the measure of a good father. And, they do not need things

74

— your children need the personhood of the father and the mother. They need personal involvement. You cannot substitute dollars for daddies, or for mothers.

In the very nature of things, children look to the father as the symbol of authority and respect. When they are not taught and do not learn from an adequate, respectful, authoritarian figure in childhood, they do not learn obedience to authority and to structure. They do not learn the basic laws of life. They have to live in the framework of an orderly society that has law, rules and regulations. They are in rebellion against police — against the establishment — against any restrictions. They rebel if they cannot express their emotions and get complete gratification. They do not realize the basic principle— you have to earn what you get in life — they want to grab it like a child, and give nothing in return. Today fathers are not giving their children love balanced with discipline, and authority balanced with sound reason. They are giving them abuse — erratic punishment — or complete neglect. That is our problem.

I know a lot of people — in their twenties and thirties — who are still in rebellion. They still have not learned the basic principle of respect for authority — of being cared for, and yet, being disciplined. I see them by the way they dress — by the way they react on the jobs. They want something for nothing all the time. They want the shortcut — the easy way. If you can make $2 million dealing in drugs, do it, get it and get out! They have thought the only value in life is to have things money, houses, cars. Daddies or dollars!

AN AGE-OLD PROBLEM

It is an age-old problem. We turn back the pages: here is David — that was his problem. He started as a shepherdboy and went to the top. He became king. He

75

had a palace, power, prestige, luxury — everything this world could give. But, his own son was in rebellion against him. When it was all over, David wept and said, O son, I would have died in your place if I could. What joy was there to gain the kingdom and sit on a throne and have every physical thing in the world you can get and to have your own son die hating you and rebelling against you — rebelling against everything you stand for — wanting to take your kingdom from you.

Do you remember the inscription above the door of the old YMCA: *What shall it profit a man if he gain the whole world and lose his own son?*

What do we need to give our children as fathers and as mothers? We cannot substitute dollars and things for the roles that we must play in family life.

OUR RESPONSIBILITIES

First of all, give your children *love*. The assurance that you love them and care about them. You do not need to love what they are doing. You may say, I will always be opposed to the immoral and wrong things you are doing — I think it is a sin against God and yourself — but I will still love you. You are still mine. So, love balanced with the expectations of discipline and principles. Do not make your children feel they are wrong inside as a person. Love them.

Then second, give them *confidence*. This is the tragedy I see — fathers and mothers beat their children down saying, You are nothing— nobody — you are no good — you are a bad person. For every child that is ruined by high expectations, there are ten who are wounded and crippled in life because of our low expectations, or no expectations. So, have high expectations. Instill confidence in your children.

Then third, we would want to give them *a worthy example.* There are three things that every child is entitled to: A child is entitled to be well-born, well-bred — well-trained and well-led. If I had to pick the most important, I would say — well-led. Set an example before your child.

Daniel Webster grew up in poverty on a rocky New Hampshire farm. Captain Ebenezer Webster, his father, was working with Daniel on a rocky hillside building a rock fence when a neighbor, well-dressed, passed by on his horse. Ebenezer said to his son, There goes a noble man. He has just been elected to Congress; he is going to Philadelphia to serve under President Washington. He has made a place for himself, a great opportunity, and he gets $6 a day. Do you know why he is going? He had an education.

His father dropped his head and said. If I had had an education early on, I would be riding to Philadelphia — I would be making my place there, too. But I did not get an education. I am destined to be a slave the rest of my life — to work out a hard living on this rocky farm. I will never have a chance to make anything of my life. Daniel Webster said he cried as he saw the sadness in his father's face — old before his time because he had had to work on this farm just to make a living.

The father kept on talking; Daniel, I want you to make something of your life — I want you to be somebody — I want you to get an education. Son, your mother and I will not buy any new clothes. We will wear these same old clothes another year. We have gathered all the money we have and I have put a second mortgage on the farm. I have enough money to send you to college. I want to give you a better chance in life than I had.

Daniel said that night in his attic room he could not sleep because he was so excited about going to college. But downstairs, neither did his daddy sleep. His daddy had put the shackles back on his wrists and determined he would work the rest of his life and die

77

enslaved to debt in order for his boy to get an education.

When you go to the halls of Congress today and hear about Daniel Webster, the silver-tongued orator who shaped the destiny of this land, just remember that Godly father, a daddy who loved and cared about his son, and know that it is Ebenezer Webster that is being honored in the annals of history — a God-fearing daddy who set an example and opened the way for his son. Daniel Webster himself said, My father — yes, he is the noblest gentleman and the greatest hero I have ever known in life.

OUR FATHER

We have talked about our fathers — now let's talk about our Father — our Heavenly Father. We are all sons and daughters of the Heavenly Father who loves us and gave Himself for us. We can say I have made such a mess of my life— and He says, I forgive you. I have sinned; I have not been a very good mother, father, boy or girl, son or daughter. And he says, I forgive you.

The greatest story of the New Testament is the prodigal son; but it is not the story of the prodigal son. It is the story of the loving father who said, Come back — I will put the ring on your finger — I will kill the fatted calf — we will rejoice — my son who was lost is found — my son who was dead is alive.

That is the invitation I give today— if you want to come to the Lord — if you want to be a Christian — if you want to come as a Christian to join the church to move your letter — to come for baptism.

Whatever it is that you need to do — will you do it now!

OUR OTHER MOTHERS

Ex. 2:1-10; Acts 7:20-21

In which time Moses was born and was exceeding fair and nourished up in his father's house three months: And when he was cast out Pharaoh's daughter took him up and nourished him for her own son.

This refers to one of the most decisive events in human history. You could take the fifteen greatest battles of all the world, someone has said, and yet all of those battles combined together have not affected and influenced the stream of human history like this single event that took place 3,000 years ago and is referred to in these little verses here.

The occasion was during the time of bondage of the children of Israel. The people of God under the pressure of the Egyptian taskmasters, had labored and suffered much. The day came when the Hebrew children were reproducing and growing so fast that Pharaoh feared that they would outnumber the Egyptians. So he sent out an edict that all male Hebrew children would be slaughtered.

When this edict went out there was a devout Hebrew couple who had a little boy born to them. This mother's name was Jochebed; and when she looked upon her own flesh, her own son, she could not see him killed. With great faith in her heart she believed that God had a destiny and a purpose for this little one. God did not send him into this world for naught.

So, with a mother's faith, she kept him and nourished him and hid him in the closet and hid him behind the curtain. But, as the time passed, this little fellow grew and grew and in three months he was noisy and crying and she began to fear for his life.

Then it was an awesome decision was made. Jochebed, the mother of Moses said. We must send him out somewhere. We cannot keep him at home. We could hide him down in the bulrushes — and maybe we can keep him there for awhile on the banks of the River Nile. So they put the child in a little ark of bulrushes daubed with pitch, like a little boat, and the baby was cradled in the water among the bulrushes. The sister Miriam was set to watch over the baby to make sure that nothing harmed him — that no animals came to disturb the child.

Then, one day a terrifying sight. Here came Pharaoh's daughter down to the river to bathe — at this exact spot. Here she came with all of her servants and maids. As they neared the water's edge, the baby cried out — and I think Miriam must have felt her heart leap into her throat as she thought, That is the end.

But something happened in the heart of Pharaoh's daughter. For when they brought the baby up to her she looked at it and said, Why, it is one of the Hebrew children. And she — not married and without a child of her own — but with that mother's love that beat in her heart, reached out and claimed that child — one not her own — and she became the other mother to Moses. Jochebed, the physical biological mother, and then Pharaoh's daughter — Thermutis was her name, according to a very ancient legend and recorded by Josephus in his account of that period, took this little one and made him her son, and was like a mother to him.

So, shaped by the faith of Jochebed and the love of Thermutis, Moses grew up in the court of Pharaoh to become the deliverer of the children of Israel — the greatest of all the prophets — the one who received the Ten Commandments from the Lord — the one who fed the stream that led to the coming of the Savior, Jesus Christ, into the world. I say to you, these two women had more influence in shaping history than perhaps the fifteen greatest battles that were ever fought in human history.

So, we pay tribute to our mothers. First of all, we pay tribute to mothers of the flesh — our biological mothers. Our hearts just overflow with the joy of every remembrance that we have of that mother, living or dead, this day. We pay tribute to that mother and that mother's faith.

But then, I want you to use your imagination and think of *the other mothers* that have touched your life — other women who loved and cared, who reached forth the tender hand of a mother's love. For example, the nurse in the hospital — like Florence Nightingale. Born of wealthy English parents while they were on holiday in Italy, Florence Nightingale was named after the city where she was born.

Coming back to England as a young woman, and dissatisfied with just the social life of the day and what wealth could offer her, she gave herself as a nurse and attended the only nursing school of that day. It was started by a minister's wife who brought girls and women into her home and taught them how to care for the sick. They were ordained as deaconesses in the Church and they went out to serve not to be called nurses, but deaconesses.

Later, Florence Nightingale went to serve in the Crimean War in southern Russia with 22 other deaconesses. They went into the hospitals in the war-torn areas, ministering to the soldiers. So great was her influence that grown men sobbed at the very

81

sight of her, and kissed the bedsheet when her shadow passed over it. So tender was her loving care as she laid her hand on a fevered brow, it was like a mother speaking words of hope and encouragement to a dying boy. She became known as the "Lady of the Lamp" as she walked through the wards at night. Florence Nightingale was another mother.

Other mothers — we can think of many who came to us in the hours of need and ministered to us. Nurses — social workers, teachers — women who come to give what doctors call TLC — giving tender loving care to some child — doing that which medicine cannot do.

I think of the hands of other mothers who reached forth to guide and direct in the classroom — to swing open the doors of opportunity and hope to boys and girls. I think of the little "lady of Possum Trot," she was called. She was born an aristocrat on a Southern cotton plantation with five older sisters all of whom were the belles of the day and enjoyed the mint julep life of that cotton plantation — but not this one.

Her name was Martha Berry; and she gave herself to higher things and became another mother to thousands and thousands of boys and girls. There came to the steps of her house three boys on a Sunday. She called them in and read Bible stories to them and said, Come back next Sunday. They came back, and they brought their sisters. They came back the next Sunday and they brought their friends. And Martha Berry started a Sunday School.

When her father died, he left her 15,000 acres of forest land in northern Georgia, and there she built the Berry Schools which today make up one of the great schools of our country. Thousands of boys and girls have worked their way through school there. Martha Berry, the inspiration of it all — another mother who reached forth her hand and opened the doors of

82

opportunity for boys and girls.

But we think of one who opened the very gates of heaven for hundreds of boys and girls right here at Walnut Street Baptist Church — Clara Nussbaum.

Gyne Alton Duncan recalled 35 years ago when, as a six-year-old boy, he walked up the steps and into her Sunday School department. There, under her leadership, he found the Lord — he found a direction in life — he found a place of business and a family— he found the chairmanship of the deacons of this church — he found a place of usefulness and service. Just a testimony to another mother who had no children of her own, but she gave her life for others.

I am speaking to many people. Maybe you have no physical children of your own — but you can be another mother, another father, and cast forth a life of influence to shadow and give a direction and open the very doors of heaven for some boy or girl. That is the greatest investment you can make in life.

You can pile the stocks and bonds high on your desk and feed your money into a bank account, and all of the things in this life will fade away and rust and decay as nothing. But what you plant in the life of a boy or girl lives on forever. Only human personality is eternal; and only that which we do for God in the life of the human being has eternal significance.

So — we salute this day every other mother who, with love like Pharaoh's daughter, gives herself to somebody else.

That is what the church is all about — we are the servant Church — we are the ministering church — we are trying to give ourselves to others through many means and ways.

HOPE FOR THE HOME

SAVING OUR FAMILIES IN
A PAGAN WORLD

Exodus 10:8-11

Newsweek magazine had a 20-page feature on "Saving the Family." *McCall's* magazine carries the findings of a survey they made in religion and morality— a survey to which 60,000 women responded— the largest response ever to any kind of survey.

Why so much attention on the family? Because there are such radical changes taking place in the families of our country—there are so many pressures on the family. And, for a decade now, there are those who have been pulling their hair and giving us statistics, frightening us by saying the family is gone — it is in trouble. What is happening? I want us to look at some of those things now.

THE PROBLEM

First of all, let us see the radical changes that are taking place. Perhaps, in this generation, the family pattern is changing in America more than it has in all the centuries put together. There is a changing structure of the family.

Sociologists tell us the *nuclear family* is the first organization of mankind and was the first basic building block of society. The nuclear family, basically, is the traditional concept. Dad is the breadwinner — getting up, going off to work, making the living. Mother is the homemaker, staying at home, making the home. Then, around the table, the dependent children. This has been the basic unit of society. But do you realize that is not the actual normal family structure today?

The statisticians say this: Only seven percent of the people in America today live in that kind of household.

What has happened? Newsweek gives these statistics. There are 56 million family units in our country — 22 million, or 40 percent of these are families without children. They may be young families without children. They may be older families, man and wife, whose children are gone; they are grown.

They tell us there are 11 million of these families where the mother is working as a breadwinner, also. And there are 9 million or 16 percent — one of every seven families — headed by a single. This may be a single parent due to death or divorce, or it may be two sisters living together, or it may be three working girls, all of them single, sharing an apartment. But we must recognize these are family relationships, family units. They may not be families of blood or families of flesh, but they are families that relate in the interpersonal relationships of a family.

When I talk about a family, I am talking about all of these. If you have a home and there is anybody living in that home with you — if you are not living just by yourself, then I am talking to you. Whether you have children or not — whether you are married or not — we are talking about this unit that forms the basis of society — the family.

Now, what are some of the *destructive* forces at work trying to destroy the family and this intimate relationship? In the *McCall's* survey, 60,000 women put three at the very top. They said the first and major destructive force is the disintegration and breakdown of family life itself. Secondly, they said there is the *influence of movies, television, books,* the gross immorality. We are being drowned in a cesspool of immorality, affecting not only the adults but also the children.

The third major factor is the example of adults to children. This is a major factor in the high escalating rate of teenage pregnancies. We could go on — the sheer materialism, absorption with things on the part of adults, peer pressure from other children — all kinds of forces at work in our society. I think it was pretty well summed up by a Phoenix mother of three teenagers: It is hard to tell kids what is right and wrong with everything they see — when the movies, television, magazines and books promote living together, sex, adultery and nudity. But, she says, no one who believes in God can say these things are moral.

So the family is under attack, everybody agrees to this. The structure is changing, the pressures are out there. Now—can we save the family in this pagan world?

Well, God came in a miraculous way and just snatched the families of the Hebrew people out of Egypt and delivered them. He took them across the river and said, We will get you out of Egypt and all the fleshpots of Egypt and your bondage and slavery. We will deliver you. And God delivered them.

I do not think God is going to come down and somehow miraculously snatch us out of this world and deliver us from it. We are in Egypt, and I do not believe we can get away from Egypt, although some try. Not long ago there came through Louisville a group of Mennonites. They had sold all their farmland in Indiana and were on their way to South America to undeveloped primitive land. Why? We are trying to get our families away from the worldly influence. They do not believe

87

in television. They do not believe in mechanization. They do not believe in all the materialism. They said. This is the way — we will go into the jungles of South America and get away from this world.

We read stories about families that just threw in the towel in New York City — tired of the asphalt and pavement, the fast-paced life, and they went out in the north woods. There they built a little cabin and isolated themselves completely. I am not sure that is the way to do it, if we could. I do not think our Christian faith is something to be lived separate and apart from the world. I do not think God intends for us to get our religion and then isolate ourselves. Leave me alone now and don't let anything contaminate me — I will withdraw.

I think God intended for us to stay right here in the world and, in the world, live out our faith—build Christian families — and set Christian examples in the world. I believe that. So, let's take a look at this.

HOPE FOR THE FAMILY

In spite of all the discouraging statistics — there is a lot of hope for the family. We cite the divorce statistics on one side— but do you realize that two of every three people who marry stay married all their lives! And 92 percent of the children in America today are raised in a family setting — and 86 percent are still in two-parent households. So, we can turn statistics around and say it is not as devastating as you think. Look at the other side.

The great thing I see in this survey by *McCall's* magazine is this — that religious faith — Christian idealism, Christian commitment and the Christian family — is alive and well in America! Though the secular family may be in trouble.

Listen to what the survey says. Of the 60,000 women

who answered, 96 percent said they believed in God and they prayed — and 56 percent of those women reported they had a born again experience with Jesus Christ.

The survey also indicated the high moral standards and high sense of responsibility — 99 percent of these women answered, It is the responsibility of the parent in the home to teach morals to the children. As one Phoenix housewife said, If a child has gone wrong, it is a parent's fault — not the church, not the school, not society — not anybody else except the parent living in the home. That is where the responsibility is.

A CHRISTIAN HOME

Let's talk about a Christian home. You may not have children around the table; you can still have a Christian home. It may not be a complete nuclear family but a relationship here in a Christian home. Isn't that what we want?

One of the greatest things we can have is a Christian relationship in this the most intimate place— where we stay all the time —where we sleep — eat — have our closest relationships. If we are not going to be a Christian there, where else are we going to be Christian? We go out and act like a Christian at church, act like a Christian in business — act like a Christian out there, but if we cannot be a Christian in the home . . .

What is a Christian home? I struggled with this. How do you define it? I read about a man who had committed a horrible crime and the reporter asked him. What in the world went wrong here? I don't know — I was raised in a Christian home.

Now, what did this criminal mean? Did he mean a Christian home in contrast to Moslem? Or did he mean he believed in the Ten Commandments and a Golden Rule and being a good neighbor?

89

Or did he believe there was a Bible out on the table and we read the Bible together? Or we went to church all the time? I have known some folks who went to church and had the Bible on the table but they were as mean as they could be — harsh, unkind, brutal — vicious.

I think, first of all, a Christian home is one that has in it a Christian atmosphere. You walk in and just feel it. You walk into this church and somebody says, I just feel like this is a loving, caring church. It is not the way we stand, or sit down, or the order of service we have. It is a feeling — people are smiling and seem happy and they greet you and they sing. There is a relaxed atmosphere here. I get the atmosphere that here are people who care when they sing, *Sweet, sweet spirit.*

That is what I am talking about in a family or a home. A Christian home has an atmosphere in it that is Christian. In Galatians 5, Paul talks about the fruits of the spirit; these are the marks of Christian living. It is love, hope, peace, joy and freedom and forgiveness. It is not griping, complaining, faultfinding, putting down. There is an atmosphere that is different, I guess it is the atmosphere of love — not the kind of bogus, physical, Hollywood love — but the kind of love that is rooted in Jesus Christ — the kind of love that Paul says; Husbands, love your wives as Christ loved the church. A pretty high standard. Love, interpreted in ways we can understand it, is acceptance of each other. A Christian home is where people accept each other as they are.

There has to be some *acceptance*. Accept me for the good and accept me for my weaknesses. Love me for the virtues, the admirable things. Love me even when you see the dark side, and accept that. Acceptance — that is what love really is —when a boy can bring home his bad report card, give it to his folks and know he will be

90

dealt with fairly and reasonably and not be beaten or abused. There will probably be some settling on the report card — you've got to get to work here — but he is not afraid and tears it up and says he lost it and has to lie about it — that sort of an acceptance.

Acceptance. Accepting a four-year-old to be a four-year-old and not expecting it to be eight — or the eight-year-old to act like a sixteen-year-old— or a sixteen-year-old to act like a twenty-five-year-old — or a twenty-five-year-old to act like you are acting after years of maturity and experience.

I think it also means *care*. Love means caring about some one, really, and telling them you care.

I am saying, You could have your name on a church roll. You can say, I have accepted the plan of salvation — I have signed my name to Jesus Christ —I'm committing myself to him and I know I am going to heaven. But you will still be unChristian and not have a Christian home if you do not know what it is to have love there that is acceptance, care, self-giving as Christ loves his church and died for it.

The second characteristic of the Christian home is *tenderness*. The scripture calls this kindness. Kindness in the way we deal with each other. We are suffering today with what we call child abuse — little children beaten, abused, broken bones, but is that any worse than the abuse we have of twisting and warping a child's personality? We put them down—tell them they cannot do anything — destroy their self-image — their self-confidence, and they grow up withered and afraid in the world.

The trouble with wife beaters — there are men who would not beat their wife, physically, but they abuse their wife and put her down and say she hasn't got any sense. And wives do the same thing! There are women called castrating wives who, by their

91

viciousness, would cut him down until he loses every sense of his manliness and self-confidence he has to have to go into the world and fight the day to day battles. There has to be kindness and tenderness in a home for it to be Christian.

And then I think there has to be *security*. That is what marriage is all about. It is a commitment for life — so that when you commit yourself to each other you can say, There is one thing we can be secure about —we have each other. This means there is a kind of physical economic security. We can face anything if we just have each other. I have you — you have me. We can lose our jobs — we can be shifted around — have adversities — but there is a security that comes physically to us.

Then there ought to be an *emotional security*. When we are hurting and in trouble, emotionally. We have somebody who lovingly cares for us. Don't think that just because you are a Christian and read your Bible and pray every day, that solves all the emotional problems of life. The best Christians can get depressed and discouraged. Paul did. We can have depression, discouragement, disheartenment. Marriage is supposed to give us that security — somebody is beside us who is going to care about us and prop us up when we need it.

There ought to be *moral security* in a home. By that I mean a husband ought to have the moral security to be able to leave town and know that his wife is going to be faithful to him while he is gone — no need to worry about that. Or the woman can have the moral security to know that when her husband goes to a convention he is not going to be immoral. Or he is not going to fall in love with his secretary or run off with her. That is what marriage is all about. That is what the home is all about — to give this kind of security to the two parties, and the children who need the security to grow into responsible well-balanced adults.

Finally, I think a Christian home should have *faith*. — Faith in Jesus Christ the Lord of your life. You cannot have a Christian home without a commitment to Jesus Christ. We can set forth all these ideals but you cannot accomplish them without the help and power of Jesus Christ in your life, because these ideals are beyond human and physical attainment. It is only by his power that you can have a Christian home.

So, it gets down to a very personal issue. If you want a Christian home, you start out first, and you be the Christian. There is not a family situation or a human relationship but that can be made better by the injection of your Christian personality into it. If you struggled with yourself and became a better Christian it would improve the situation.

Would you let it start with you?

HOPE FOR THE HOME

WHY GOD GAVE CHILDREN PARENTS

Joshua 24:14-18

Why did God establish the family? God gave us a spiritual family in the church that is a divine institution; and He gave us a physical family in the flesh produced by holy matrimony — marriage. And what I have to say will certainly apply spiritually in the family of faith, and it will apply also in the family of the flesh.

A preacher by the name of Lee Bristol tells about being in Penn Station in New York City when a man, unshaven and disheveled, said to him, Sir, you look like you are friendly — would you talk to me a minute? Yes, I have a minute. So the man told a tragic story of a wasted life and finished by saying. There is not a single person in all this world that cares whether I live or die right now — not a person. Mister, I don't know your name and you don't know mine — but, would you do me a favor? For the next couple of weeks, would you just remember me and think about me. If I could just know there is somebody in this world thinking about me as a human being, it would be worth a million dollars to me. Would you do that? Yes, I will. And before he could say anything else, the man just faded away — nameless and unknown — into the crowd. He was reaching out — grasping— for the thing we all must have or we cannot survive. We have to have somebody that cares about us. If you do not have anybody in all this world that cares about you as a human being, you cannot make it — I cannot make it.

That is why God gave us a family. That is why God said, It shall be so that there shall be a man and a woman and they shall join themselves and bring into this world a child — and that is to be the family — that is to be the place where somebody will always care for this person as a human being. The family is the place we go where we always know they will receive us and care about us. We can be on the other side of the world; regardless of what the circumstances are, if we are a part of the family, we can say, I know there is somebody this day caring about me.

The ideal that God set up is for a family to be made up of two people — a husband and a wife. But I recognize there are many families, by different circumstances, such as one parent families and I want to say something very important to you: Do not give up. Do not say you cannot perform the parenting responsibility effectively. The task of parenting can be done by one as well as two — you do not have to have two people to build a good family.

Now, it is harder where one has to do it all; but the functions are the same and can be carried out by one person. Do not be discouraged — do not throw in the towel —do not give up. If you are in a one-parent family situation because of death or divorce or abandonment — whatever it is— get hold and say, By the grace of God, I can do it! You can look around and see many one-parent families that are doing a good job with the family. I can see a lot of two-parent families that are going down the tube because one, or both, are doing a poor job at parenting.

Making a home is much like making a garden. You get a plot of ground — you plow it and prepare the soil — you plant the seed. Pretty soon the seed sprout and come up and you have a crop growing; and you cultivate and nurture it. You do not abandon it; you nurture it to bring forth fruit. Building a family is the same thing, two people get together — plow the ground — sow the seed — and up comes life. Sometimes we say it does not need cultivating. Just let it grow. Abandon your garden, and the weeds will take it. Abandon your family, and the devil will take it.

There is something very obvious in this analogy. You cannot do it yourself — if making a family and making a garden are alike. You cannot make a garden by yourself. Oh, you do the plowing —you have to do your part. But then, the miracle — something supernatural has to happen. God comes in to give the sunshine and the rain and the life of the seed to bring forth new life. The author of life has to give life to that seed and bring it forth. And, in the same way— and recognize it — you are dependent upon God if you are going to make a family. It is God who gives you this little child — it is the power of life from God that brings that seed into the world — it is God's gift. So start from the beginning and make God a part of your family.

What do children *need* when they come into your family? Why did God give children parents? We could make a list as long as my arm — but let's just hit the very essentials.

God gave children parents *to provide for their physical needs.* A baby is born into the world not able to care for itself — feed itself — clothe itself — forage for itself — protect itself. So physical care is the most obvious need. Many of us work at it and do a good job in providing physical care. We feel if we have brought home the bacon, built the house, bought the clothes, and paid the bills, we have done our job. But that is not enough. The needs are more than just physical security.

A child needs love. We all need to be loved and we

need to express love. At the center and core of the family there has to be love if there are to be children nurtured into full maturity as God wills it. One person can give that love. It is good to have two people — it is good to have a family of several people. But you can be the person in the family that gives the love that is needed. You can do it.

Now, we are talking about a family, whether it is a family of the flesh or the spiritual family of the church that God has given us. We are children in the family of God in the church. God gave us this church because He did not intend for us to live the solo life spiritually any more than He intended for us to live the solo life physically apart from everybody. We came into the church because we need love — we need to give love and be loved. The great witness of the New Testament is that God is a Father who loves us as children. We are brothers and sisters and joint-heirs with Jesus Christ to God our Father in the church.

This is where single parents find support groups for someone in their family. They find a father figure or a mother figure in a Sunday School teacher or in Scouting, in the choirs, in school, or among relatives, grandparents, aunts and uncles. They bring in someone else in a love relationship — they already have in the family of faith. They find a second person to help them in parenting — to give the love.

Children also need discipline. What does the word mean? The word, *discipline,* comes from the word, *disciple* — same root, same word, same idea. A *disciple* is a *learner.* So there is teaching and learning. Discipline is not just corrective punishment for wrongdoing. Discipline is supposed to be a learning procedure to teach a child how to live and get along in the world.

You see, life has fences around it. Do not trespass.

These fences protect the rights of other people — the right of society and the obligation of society. As an adult, a child is going to be thrown into that world of fences. That adult will have to use some self-discipline not to climb over that fence. So, we have to start early — we have to put little fences around a child and say, These are the rules— these are the limits. You cannot be permissive and say, There are no fences— let them do as they please — let them go. Discipline is for the purpose of teaching a child how to live and get along with other people.

Then, God disciplines us —He has some fences around our lives, too, and when we climb over those fences, God sometimes has to discipline and punish us. And some of the things that happen to us— that is the discipline of God dealing with you and me as children in his family.

Grady Wilson of the Billy Graham team was asked: Did your mother or daddy ever spank you? His answer: We had a strap in the kitchen — it hung on a nail right under the sign: I need thee every hour. That is discipline — physical discipline. But when that physical discipline is carried to an extreme without teaching and without kindness in it, we have brutality. And we see a lot of battered children today. A boy, who was picked up unconscious, had 67 bruises on him. They charged the father with child abuse. The father's defense was, I believe in discipline and he is a bad boy. You can do that physically, or you can take rules, or your Bible — yes, even religion — and beat the child to death— abuse them with it. That is not discipline.

There are some points about discipline that are important. First, *love* needs to stand out there in front. I am disciplining you but, above all, I love you. Secondly, it needs to be *honest* disciplining, fair disciplining. You cannot demand one standard for your children and another for yourself. You have to set an example of

99

fairness before them. And then, discipline must also be *consistent*. You just cannot ride with your emotions. You get angry and you discipline — you are not angry and you are lax. You cannot waiver back and forth like that. So— discipline is for teaching. And every child needs it.

Then, *children need self-esteem*. I want to bring my child into this world equipped to live in it — to meet the problems of it. That child has to have self-esteem to feel that they are worth something — that they are somebody. Now, I can either destroy that or I can build it as I have this tender plant growing in the garden of my family. Always criticizing — condemning —belittling — laughing at — making fun of — scoffing at a child will destroy a child's self-esteem. When they get out into the world, they will not be able to cope with the problems of life because they have no confidence in themselves.

There was a ministerial student — mark you, a ministerial student — who felt that God had called him to preach and he stuttered terribly. His stuttering was due to the fact that, as a child, he had a minor speech defect. He had a father that was a Ph.D and a highly educated mother; yet that father and mother mimicked his speech defect, made fun of him and ridiculed him, thinking that was the way to cure him. Instead, it made him stutter so badly that he was afflicted and never could fulfill the purpose that he thought God had for him as a preacher.

Get off your child's back and get on your child's team! Get with him! Get with her! A little cartoon here in the office is a picture of a little child with this underneath, I'm somebody, because God don't make no junk! God made a beautiful, wonderful thing in a child and it is our purpose to try to give them self-esteem — a sense of worth that they are somebody.

And that is our purpose in the church, in the family of God. Paul says we are all a part of the body of Christ. One is a finger, another is an eye — but you cannot say the eye is more important than the finger, or the finger is more important than the eye. We all have our part— our gifts — our place. We are all somebody. Self-esteem — that is what the family of the flesh and the family of faith can give us.

What should I want to give my children? If God were to say, Write three or four things you want to give your child and I will grant these to you — what would you say? What is the most important thing you would like to give your child? Your business, your calling, your vocation? A minister was asked to talk to the sixth grade class about how to find your place in life — your job, your task. He passed out some cards and said, Write on here any question — anything you want to ask me — and I will try to answer. One card came back, My father is a dentist. My father wants me to be a dentist. I don't want to be a dentist. Can you help?

It is true that a child in the sixth grade does not know what he wants to do; and, one thing sure, about that age he does not want to do anything his father wants him to do. He is at that age where he is beginning to say, If daddy wants it, I don't. So do not take that too seriously. However, I think if the father knew the boy felt that way, maybe he would change his relationship. Do we want to make them over just like we are — to fulfill the things we missed in life? No. The thing I would like to give my child is not my job or my unfulfilled hopes or the things I missed in life.

The first thing I would want to give my child is a *vital personal faith in God through Jesus Christ.* A vital religious experience — so they will be able to cope with success, failure, pain, suffering, and even death itself. They will be able to take it all in stride, because they have a solid foundation for faith in God.

101

The second thing is *a vital church relationship.* I want to tie them into a church that is meaningful — I do not care what the label is. The day is over when we scrap over the label and argue about the denomination. Encourage them to find a church in which they can express themselves — a church that needs them and one that they need. If they make their friends with other Christian parents and other couples that have the same values and ideals — if they get that circle around them, that will be the support group to help them when times get tough. I want to give them a church home — not make them join my church instead of that girl's church or that boy's church. I am going to say, Get in a church where you will really be active where it will mean something to you — where your faith will grow.

Then the third thing I want to give them— *the goal of developing their own God-given abilities,* and use those abilities to serve their fellowman — not to fulfill my goal, but have their own goal — to discover their abilities and develop them.

They may want to be a garbage collector and that is their ability. That is all right — if they will do that job to serve others and realize that the fulfillment of life is not in the money you make or the prestige of the title, but how you satisfy and develop the gifts God has given you and use them to the glory of God to serve your fellowman.

Then, the last thing I would like to give — *the confidence to do it.* I believe in them; they are somebody. Christ believes in them. He died for them. Friends believe in them — and they can go and do it. Those are the gifts every parent would like to give a child.

So—what are we going to do about it? Joshua stood before the people and said, Choose ye this day — decide what you are going to do right now, today. Every day is election day; not once a year, once every four years. Every day, we stand at the crossroads and elect to go one way or another about something. I am talking now about your own life — about your family — about your church — about your marriage. There are some decisions you face.

Think with me right now. Ten years from now, what decisions will you wish you had made today? I wish I had decided on that first Sunday in May that I had made a decision this way, or that way. Then do it, today! Procrastination is always the thief that takes away from us the great gifts that God wants to give to us — the blessings He wants to give us. We put it off — I will do it tomorrow. No — today. Choose ye this day, Joshua said. Now is the decision time.

You say. I am not free to make my choice —there are others involved. If I had the cooperation of my wife — my husband — you don't know my family situation. No, but God does, and God is ready to help you. You can have a transforming spiritual experience yourself that will give you the strength, the power, the energy, and the foresight and persistence that will get you on the track. You may not get somebody else in the family on the track, but you can get yourself on the track — that is a start; and that may be the solution.

A woman came to a pastor telling of their problem marriage. As the pastor listened, he decided the woman was right; the man was at fault. He was an arrogant, spoiled young man, given to fits of anger. He would sulk and then would be abusive — he was a problem — he was to blame. But the pastor was wise enough to say. I know it is not 100% his fault — it may be 90% and 10% after all, there is always another side. So he said. Do you have any religious life in your family —any at all? She said. No. I was religious, very faithful before I married— but no. Isn't God in your family now? No. God is not there — my husband speaks of God quite

103

often but not in the way you think — he uses God only as a curse word. The pastor said, You cannot be responsible for what your husband does; he will have to stand before God himself. But you are responsible for what you do. I want you to start a religious life in your family. Start with grace at the table — just saying a prayer at the table with him.

That night before they started to eat she said, Jim, I would like to have a prayer and thank God for this food, thank God for our home, thank God for you and our marriage. He did not say anything, and she prayed. The next morning she prayed, and that evening. He just sulled. Finally, after about two weeks, he said, I am supposed to be head of this house — if anybody prays around here, I am going to pray. With that, he dropped his head and prayed. And that broke the dam. They prayed together and they talked it out. They found their place in church and he found his place before the Lord. But she had to do it herself.

I am saying to you: You have been putting it off —I cannot do it by myself. Yes, you can. You can do it. God looks for you to do what you can do — whatever that means. Whether it means your public dedication to Jesus Christ — or moving your membership and getting in a church— or the renewal of your vows — whatever it is — Do it.

THE FAMILY THAT ENDURES

Psalm 127

A television network recently presented a documentary on the American family. For almost a year they observed the Laud family. The documentary, showing all facets of life, portrayed a family that was going to pieces — unraveling. The pressures of modern society developed some awesome conclusions about the loss of family life. The family, as we have known it, is disappearing from the American scene.

Ann Royce, a writer with the *New York Times,* wrote her own impressions of the documentary. I want you to hear it carefully, for she puts her finger on the real problem with the Laud family.

"When sorting through the experience of viewing the Lauds, my first realization was that all the avenues of culture, as I have understood them, were missing from their family life. If there is such a thing as negative culture, or culture minus, the Lauds have it. The blaring sound of Rock is the high point of creativity in the family. There are no crafts, no basket-making, no pottery, no weaving — although a lot of fuss over clothes. But they were purchased and not made.

"There was no religion. No threatening Jehovah; no merciful Mary; no sense of the beyond; or the Talmud; or the catechism.

"There is no avenging sensibility. No real moral right or wrong. No sense of judgment of good or bad weighing over the family. In strict traditional societies everyone knows the rules — the punishment for breaking them — what they can do and cannot do.

"I think the Lauds have escaped the small town morés of early America. They have been educated and led into a large vacuum, and like the rest of us, they are cast out without the structures of work and religion that used to shape our days. He have so much freedom that we are culturally Neanderthal.

"I feel badly that I can do so few things for myself, with my own hands — that I am a consumer — and my children, like me, buy before they build. I have no household gods, or any other kind to keep me civilized. And, like the Lauds, I belong to no organizations or sisterhoods.

"I feel often as if I had been set too free. Culture, if it means anything, must mean the binding of the individual to the social fabric."— And her last sentence in that article is this: "My threads are all undone."

Now Ann Royce speaks for a lot of people today who feel the very fabric of life has gone to pieces and threads are undone — especially in family life. She did not express it like an evangelical Christian. But she put her finger on every one of the problems facing the family today.

The question today: Are we going to build a family structure, a family life, like the Lauds — or like the Lord's family? The Lord has a family plan.

From the time of creation, God has set principles and guidelines for us to build an enduring family. It is God's will and purpose that a male and a female shall be joined together in a sacred union called marriage. Out of that marriage shall come children, and family life shall prepare those children to perpetuate faith, morals, traditions, and culture into the next generation. That is God's purpose in creation.

As we talk of building a family that endures, I want us to build it as you would build a house. I want us, first, to lay . . .

THE FOUNDATION

Unless there is a solid foundation, it is as though it were built on sand. When the storms of life come, I care not how good the superstructure, the storms will sweep away the sands at the foundation and the house will fall.

The verses in my text set forth the foundation. Except the Lord build the house, they that labor build in vain. The foundation stone must be personal faith — a personal commitment to Jesus Christ — a vital faith — not just a traditional faith passed from parents down to you — but a faith that is expressed and experienced every day in your own life. Except you have that foundation, you are building on sand.

That Christian faith can be expressed in the household in many ways — by simple reverence for the word of God — the use of the word of God as God speaks to the family. It is difficult in our social pattern these days to have a formal family devotional as in rural America when all the family gathered after a day's work in the field. But you can find time, certainly at meals in a simple ritual of having a blessing at the table. By what you say, and what you do, you are acknowledging God's presence — your obligation and stewardship to God — and your gratitude to God for the gift of food and your family. By word and by example, parents, lay this foundation.

But, the foundation is not an automatic assurance that you will have an enduring family — just because you walk an aisle and declare your faith in Jesus Christ and two Christian people join together and begin to produce children. You can point to the fellowship even in the church and say, There were two Christians. Their marriage has disintegrated; their family has gone to pieces.

You must build a superstructure onto that foundation. The reason we are not mature Christians — We are not full grown the minute we are saved: You have to grow in Christian virtue. It is a lifetime process of maturing, of growing and building this house.

Paul sets forth many admonitions about the character of the Christian father and mother. I think of four that express the four walls of this house. The first wall . . .

COMMUNICATION

It is so basic. There has to be communication in the family. God was the first communicator. He communicated His love to us through Jesus Christ. He communicated His love for His creation through the prophets in the Old Testament. God has communicated His love to us in our salvation experience, and in His Bible. That is the mark of the divine within us; we have the capacity of communicating back with God.

This same capacity is given to us to communicate love, affection, heartbreak, sorrow, joys and tears, one with another. How tragic that we work at communication in every other area and neglect it in our family life! We feel we do not have to worry about communicating with the family, whether it is a spouse, a mate, or children. One woman said, Huh, communication — I am married to old Stone Face. I never get any response from him.

A cartoon showed a man at the breakfast table, his newspaper laid down in utter disgust. Across the table his wife was grinning at him. She had put two pieces of bread in the toaster, then aimed it at him. The toast shot out and knocked the paper out of his hand. She had at last broken that barrier. Does this indicate to you the problems we have?

Here are some simple guidelines on communication.

Be sensitive to the other person. Sensitivity is a

108

Christian virtue. We can get so self-centered, we are insensitive to other people. Be sensitive, above all, to the ones you love most in your family relationships.

Then, listen because of who a person is, not because of what they are saying. What they are saying may be boring as can be. Sometimes your wife will rattle on about things not important to you. Or your husband comes home talking about all that is going on in the business — and you do not care about that. Or your children come to you with such silly little talk. But you are going to listen — not because of what they say but because of who they are.

Let me show you. When your boss starts telling you about his hobby — you could care less. You are bored stiff while he describes about how he raises orchids. But you listen— and ask questions — and act as if you want to know all about his orchids — because he is your boss.

If you do that out there, how much more so ought you to do it with those with whom you are inseparably tied in the family relationships of love. Listen and communicate because of who a person is.

Third, *be honest and open.* The greatest problem I face in talking with folks about their difficulties is when one says, Well, he/she gets mad and just sulks and won't say anything. How can you solve a problem if you do not say what the problem is— and the other one does not know?

One of the games married people often play is, I've got a secret — and they keep it a secret. They will not tell what has hurt them — what has upset them. They just freeze out the other person so they have to guess what is wrong. If you cannot be open and honest in your family life, where can you be open and honest? Christ talks of being without guile, being open and honest — that is the highest Christian virtue; we ought to practice it at home.

Another one: *Hear what is being said* — not what you think is said. A man comes to the table, he cuts into that steak, and takes a bite. Chewing on it, he says, Where did you get this steak? She says, What! Don't you like it? What's wrong with it? He did not say anything was wrong with it; he said, Where did you get it?

He might want to say, This is the best steak I've ever had — where did you buy it? She did not hear what he said; she jumped to the conclusion something was wrong.

I would say: We have to grow and grow and keep on growing and working at this business of communication.

The second wall . . .

DISCIPLINE

Ann Royce said, There are no rules in the Laud family. They do not know what is right, what is wrong — there is no threatening Jehovah — there is no consequence — they have lost their sense of morality. Why? Because there has been the breakdown of discipline and the attitude of total permissiveness — everything and anything goes. Let the person do "their own thing" today.

Now, I want you to balance this out. On one side we have this permissiveness — on the other side we have the battered child and abuse that goes to the other extreme. We must recognize that is wrong, certainly. But the Bible is true when it says, Train up a child in the way that he should go; and when he is old, he shall not depart from it.

The purpose of training, of discipline, is first of all to *teach the child authority.* When the child moves into the world as an adult, he has to submit to authority.

Whether he likes the authority or not —whether the rules or laws are fair or not — and whether he is in agreement or not — nevertheless, a part of living in society is to obey the laws, the rules, and submit to authority. If a child does not learn that in the home, then later on, society has to teach it to the child. And many times that means punishment, even imprisonment — trying to teach what a mother and father should have taught at home.

The second purpose of discipline is to *teach the consequences of wrongdoing.* When you do wrong, you have to suffer the consequences. Again, if you do not learn it in the home, you will learn it out in society. It is tragic if a person is an adult before learning that doing wrong brings consequences.

The third purpose of discipline is to *establish habits of right living.* We act according to habit. And the value of discipline is to establish habits that are right.

And, fourth, discipline *teaches them how to exercise responsible freedom and make responsible choices.* Regulate the behavior according to wise choices.

Discipline can be carried out in many ways. It should never be done in anger. Again, I tried to think of some guidelines on discipline:

Be *consistent* in your discipline — even though you may not be fair — you may worry about whether or not you are being fair. Authorities say, over the long run, it is not so much how extreme you are in being unfair; the important thing is to be consistent. A child grows up knowing that here are some borders, some boundaries. There is some consistency; they do not just bend with every wind or every whim.

And, *do not ask a child why he did something.* First of all the child does not know why most of the time. It was impulsive.

111

Secondly, if the child does know, he is probably not going to tell you why he did it. If he is mad at you, he will not tell you that is why he did it. He will tell some story.

Third, *do not give severe punishment.* This is something we as Christians need to hold up to the world. Do not be severe, harsh, dictatorial in your punishment. Criminologists even say this is one of the basic laws of dealing with a criminal mind.

It is not the severity of the punishment that retards them from doing evil or bad; it is the certainty of punishment — not how bad the consequences — but how certain they are. The certainty that you will be punished is far more important than the threat of bad punishment.

So, with consistency, be certain that when wrong is done, there is an accountability for it. You do not warn them — warn them— warn them, five or six times, Well, next time—well, next time — then finally, the sixth time — go ahead and punish them. Just do it the first time and begin to establish the right pattern of discipline.

Above all, in discipline, *do not punish a child in a way that humiliates the child.* That destroys the child's self-image and self-confidence. Do not put them down — you stupid child, why did you do this? Nothing can be more destructive to a child's self-image. You can say, You did a stupid thing — you are too smart to do something like that — you are such a bright, fine boy — I'm so proud of you — but this you did is bad! You can do better than that — you are going to have to be punished for it. That builds at the same time it disciplines.

And always maintain the relationship — there is nothing a child can do that can cause you not to love them. You will stand against the world with your child.

You dislike what they did, but you like them.

Discipline is important. You have failed your family; you have failed in building an enduring home, if you do not put up that wall of discipline.

And the third wall . . .

APPRECIATION

I appreciate you. Three of the most wonderful words in the English language! William James, the father of modern psychology, was very ill a long time. A friend sent him a potted azalea with a note that said, I appreciate the tremendous contribution you have made to humanity. Your work is marvelous.

William James wrote back: I want to apologize. I have made a glaring mistake in my book. I have overlooked completely one of the deepest qualities of human nature — that one of the greatest needs of humanity is to be appreciated.

Many a family withers and dries up because nobody around the household says, I appreciate you. I am proud of you. We get so focused on the negative — on pointing out the wrongs — on criticism — what's wrong with the housekeeping. What's wrong with my wife. What's wrong with my husband. What's wrong — what's wrong — and everything is wrong with the children.

It is so easy to get in the habit of saying. I am proud of you. It is so easy to get in the habit of seeing the good things, as well as the bad things. How many family lives would be changed if those in the household would determine to say something good about other members of the family every day!

It is a good meal — you look so nice — I'm so proud of you — you are the best husband a woman every had — you're a fine son

I'm so proud of you. You did a good job mowing the

lawn. I am so glad I can leave you with responsibility. You did such a good job taking care of the younger children while we were gone last night. I'm proud of you — I appreciate you.

And finally, put up the last wall . . .

ENDURING AFFECTION

. . . enduring love — love that goes on and on and on — the greatest of the Christian virtues. The Greek uses three words for love. One, *eros*, which is erotic love, a basic love, a physical attraction that brings a man and a woman together in the first place. That love will rise and fall.

Then there is *phileo* love, the love of a brother, a sister, the love of a brother for a brother. The love of friendship. This kind of love grows in a marriage. You ought to be the best of friends.

But the deepest love is the love of God, *agape*. Self-giving love, as God gave Himself through Jesus Christ. The Apostle Paul talks about this family that endures, the marriage that endures, when each one in that family loves the other one as Christ loved His church and gave Himself for it. That kind of selfless love that says, You exist in this household, not to make me happy — but I exist to make you happy. When you have that wall built out of the discipline of Christian love, day by day, you are going to build a house that endures. Four walls on a foundation that shall not be shaken.

Look at the words of B. B. McKinney:

God, give us Christian homes! Homes where the Bible is loved and taught. Homes where the Master's will is sought, Homes crowned with beauty thy love hath wrought. God, give us Christian homes.

A FAMILY ENDURES

Colossians 3:12-21

Martin Luther, father of the modern reformation, writes about the wedding feast at Cana and the miracle of turning water into wine in terms of his personal experience. Martin Luther was an old bachelor monk, who lived in a cold damp monastery as was the tradition of his church. But breaking with that tradition, he decided that man was not made to live alone. He studied the scripture and he became aware of the nunnery across the courtyard and one nun in particular caught his eye. Before it was all over, Martin Luther had proposed to this nun and he married her. And out of that marriage experience here is the interpretation Luther gives to the wedding at Cana and to Christ's changing water to wine.

He says, When Christ comes into the home, as He did at Cana, and into the marriage, as He came to that marriage feast — He always changes the water of life into the wine of life — sparkling, tasteful and wonderful. But if Christ is not in the home, and not in the marriage, we change the wine of life into water, and all the zest is gone, and all the joy is gone.

He said Christian marriage — holy matrimony — is a three-sided triangle: The physical side, the physical relationships; The legal side, social obligations and responsibilities to the state to be legitimatized; And tragically, many people only see or experience these two sides, because there is the spiritual side also, the third side. You cannot say then, God has joined them together, and you do not call that holy matrimony.

Vol. XIII May 27, 1982 No. 21

This is also a factor we should look at when we talk of breaking this legal and physical relationship. Were they really married in the sight of God? I am convinced that many people live together in legal marriage whom God has no more joined together than those who are just living together.

Then we said the third side, Christian marriage, forms the base of the triangle — God is in their lives and it is holy matrimony.

Now, I talk about "the family that endures" — the coming together of two people. A family is two people together. Traditionally, the family is the mother, father, and child. Today we use different terms. We talk about the nuclear family. The extended family — that may include a grandparent, an uncle, an aunt, even cousins living in a family unit. The one-parent family. So I am talking about the family in this larger sense. The family unit is the basic building block of orderly society. And it must function properly as a family in order for society to endure.

So what makes the family last? What keeps it from going on the rocks? He are terrified today with statistics about divorce — the breakup of a marriage — the breakup of families where children — runaways, delinquents — are separated from their parents — of parents abandoning their children — and abandoning responsibility.

He are also frightened by the knowledge we have, psychologically, about how inadequate we are — what failures we are — a father fails in giving the proper father-image to a child, and the damage it does to the child. This is all played up when a child goes wrong. There are analyses as to why: What is the home like — how the father, the mother, did as a parent — the mistakes they made? We look back and see the failures we made and we carry this huge burden of guilt. If I

116

could just live it over, do it over, how much better I could have been.

Let's remember this: First of all, there are no perfect children who grow into perfect adults. Every person is going to mess up their lives, one way or another, and again and again, because of the sin in their lives. It is not the blame of the father, or the mother, or the home life — it is the blame of Satan and evil in the world and in our hearts, and that is a struggle. Just because something goes wrong in the life of your child do not say, I've been a terrible failure —I am to blame.

On the other hand, there are no perfect parents. You cannot be a perfect parent! I care not how much you have learned since your children grew up, you would still make mistakes. And God does not expect us to be perfect.

These inadequacies remind me of the two dairy cows standing in the field eating grass. Down the road came the dairy truck — on the side of the truck it said, Homogenized — Pasteurized — Vitamin D Reinforced Milk. One cow said to the other, Doesn't that make you feel inadequate?

So, we are parents feeling so inadequate — how can I — in this imperfect world, with so many pressures — build a family that will endure? Well, I want to take that Christian marriage as the foundation of a house. I want to say, Building a family is like building a house.

And Paul says for one side of this house — here is one thing that will make you adequate.

LOVE

Vs. 14: Above all these things, put on *love*. Build the wall of love, first of all, in your family; and that single thing can overcome every other failure. You can be uneducated — make psychological blunders in dealing with your children— be an imperfect parent—

but through it all, you love them — that love is unquestioning— and you sustain that love in a way to say, Wherever you are, whatever you do, I will always love you — I will never reject you. I may not like what you are doing, but I love you.

Paul says that love has many facets to it. It is *kindness*. Being kind one to another. A husband is kind to a wife and a wife is kind to a husband; when children have parents who are kind to each other — not mean to each other — do not cut each other down — do not hurt each other — they see that kind of love. Parents can make lots of mistakes in a lot of ways, but the children feel secure in that kindness and love.

Love is *understanding*. To put yourself in the other person's place — to understand them and where they are coming from. So, love your child and say, I want to put myself in your place — l know what you are going through — I remember when I was your age, I know how hard it was —I know what peer pressure is.

Psychologists tell us there are two great crisis times in every human being's life. There is the crisis time that peaks in the teen years, when a child is coming out of childhood and entering into adulthood. Great physical changes take place — drives are unleashed and they are unable to handle them; therefore, they feel guilty about them. They fear being pushed out of the security where decisions have been made, where others take responsibility for their actions. Now, they make their own decisions. They are afraid; yet they want to be grown, and they blunder so badly. Parents know and recognize this, too. I am not worried about the nuclear age, or the space age, if the Lord will just get us through the teen age. That is the crisis time.

Psychologists say the other crisis time in life is the — midyears, 35 to 45. The crisis time in marriages. The crisis time physically for men. They wonder if their career has peaked — 39 and holding — right in the

118

middle — 40 years old! Life is slipping away! And they pointed out that, in most families, these crisis times cross. These parents have teenage children. Teenage children have these mid-life parents — both are going through a crisis of life at the same time.

Now — what if you have love here? Love says, I understand. Parents say, I am having troubles but I understand my children are having the worst time they will ever have in life. And teenagers say, I am having problems, but I know Mom and Dad are having problems, too. And each understands and loves the other.

So — in building a family that endures — I would say, the first wall of this house that is going to endure is *love.*

Then a second wall . . .

SHARING

In building my house on the foundation of Christian marriage, this wall should be *sharing.* A family is a relationship where every member shares in it.

That is a real family! And that is the way it is supposed to be. Even the least one shares in some responsibly — some kind of sharing — this is your part of the responsibility. Then, as you grow up — the husband says, This is my responsibility, this is my job. Then the mother — this is my responsibility, these are the things I do. A lot of families go on the rocks because they do not define responsibilities and live up to them.

Now — sharing in decisions — communicating with each other. It is our money and we join together. One way of getting control and power in a family is to control the money. That wrecks the marriage — using power to beat the other one into submission.

First, love, and then, sharing together — sharing decisions, responsibilities, sharing with each other your love, your money, your affection.

And then the third wall I would build over here. . .

DISCIPLINE

So often the discipline is for the good of the parent rather than for the good of the child. They use discipline to vent their anger, to get rid of their tensions, to get rid of their frustrations. They get mad, blow up and discipline the child. It does not do the child a bit of good — it does the parent a lot of good. That is the wrong kind of discipline.

The man's wife was cooking a very special new recipe and a wonderful dinner. She had fixed a beautiful salad; she had vegetables ready to put on the stove and a special meat recipe. And her little boy was just giving her fits. He would run through the kitchen — Mommy this — Mommy that — she had told him again and again to stay out of the kitchen, to let her alone so she could cook supper. But he came tearing through again — knocked against the table and knocked the salad to the floor — it went everywhere — and in anger she grabbed the poker and started after him. He went running out the door, down the front steps and under the house as far as he could crawl! She crawled in after him, but she decided this was a very undignified thing for her to be doing. I will let my husband take care of that boy!

The husband came home, and he was very well trained. Go discipline your son! Do something about your son! So he crawled under the house, looking all around, until he saw two bright eyes peering around a pillar, and a soft voice said; Paw, is she after you, too?

Discipline is necessary. As parents we need to learn how to discipline properly. What is the purpose of discipline, anyway? Discipline is to teach a child that they cannot do things that are wrong and not acceptable in society and not be punished. So, when they get older, they can use their freedom responsibly.

They can restrain their impulses and not let them loose any way they want.

If we do not discipline and teach a child, when that child becomes an adult, society will discipline them. They are going to arrest them — they are going to jail them — they are going punish them and say. You cannot do these things. That is the purpose of discipline.

How do we teach through discipline? I ran across something a criminologist said, and he proved his point. He said it is not the severity of the punishment, but the certainty of punishment that retards criminal acts. You can say you are going to the death chair; that does not stop it. You could say ten years in prison — that would be about as much deterrent. . ."as would be necessary." It is not the severity, but the certainty. And we have lawlessness today because of the lack of certainty of penalty. People say, I can do it and get by!

Apply this to children — it is not the severity of the punishment. We see the tragedy of child brutality and battered children — this is severe discipline and that is not what you need for discipline. You can have very light penalty, but *certain* penalty. If you do it — not the sixth time after I have told you but the first time — there is a penalty, and you learn you cannot do it without paying for it.

As I put up this third side of the house, I would say, Do not forget in disciplining to go back to love and praise; never demean the child. Do not say, You are a bad child — but, What you *did* was bad. You are too good, too fine a child — you are not a bad child, but you did a bad thing. And I will always love you. Praise, lift up in praise. Do not destroy their self-esteem.

And then, *forgive*. Susanne Wesley, the mother of John and Charles Wesley, was one of the great mothers of history. When asked, How many times should you forgive a child — she said. As many times as necessary!

121

Always forgiving. Always loving.

And the last side — the fourth wall . . .

GROWTH

We have to grow. If there is not growth in the family, the family will not survive. We say, Certainly, we expect growth when a little baby comes along; we want children to grow. If they do not grow, it is a tragedy. The child will grow and grow into maturity.

But what about the growth of the mother, or the father? Somehow, we think they are not supposed to grow once they are married. That is not so. The tragedy today: We have little girls playing with dolls — then we have big girls who are married but still girls, still children, playing with live babies. And marriage and parenthood are for adults.

We have boys who play games as children. They grow up and are married men and fathers and still boys playing boys games. I have to chuckle every time I go along River Road past the yacht sales place. They have a big sign saying, Toys for Men! That is almost too true to be funny. Too many men look at life as a game; and they have the responsibility of parenthood and homemaker. You must grow! Are you growing in the family? Father — mother — are you growing every day? Becoming more mature?

A woman said to the counselor: I must divorce my husband. He is driving me crazy — he assumes no responsibility for the house, the home, or the children. He never spends any time with them. He is a burden around my neck— I must take care of everything while he plays golf every moment he has free — he will not lift a finger around the house— he will not fix a thing — I have to do everything like that —when he is off on the weekends, he goes fishing with the men. The children hardly know they have a father. I am going to divorce him!

They called the man in — he was absolutely shattered! He thought he was a good father. I love my wife; I love my children — I don't believe in divorce — what is the matter? She says this — this — this about you. He had not thought about that — all right. I don't want to lose my wife— I do not want a family breakup — I will give up golf — I will quit fishing — I will do anything she wants me to do!

So the counselor got them together. He said, Don't leave me — I will give it all up. The counselor said, Maybe you do not need to give it all up — why don't you do this — you play golf at that club — why don't you take out a full membership when you play golf, take your family with you and let her and the children swim. When you come in, then you can all go in and eat dinner together. Oh, that would be heaven if he would just do it.

About fishing — the next time you go fishing, take your boys with you. I did not think they would want to go. They would love to go; and she said, And I would like to go with you, too!

Now about that work at home — instead of playing golf on your afternoon off — tell your wife, I am yours for half a day— I will sit with the children for you to go out—I will mow the lawn—I will fix the roof — whatever.

In just a moment a husband and wife grew up! They both had been children — still selfish — they had not been able to communicate and understand. They grew up! They found how to be grown and mature. We must grow!

So there is your house — the family that endures has love, sharing, discipline, growth — and a foundation — Christian marriage.

But it does not have a roof. If you live in a house

without a roof, you are in trouble. You are fine when the weather is clear, the sun is shining, and no storms in the sky. But the moment the rains come — the storm — the cold weather — you are in trouble — you cannot live in a house without a roof.

And the roof is what? Put over that house religious faith. Shelter that framework for a family that will endure with an over-arching covering — a vital, personal faith in Jesus Christ, with the word of God as a guide, and you have a house that will stand, and a family that will endure.

REDEEMING THE FAMILY

Proverbs 12:7

Let me share with you some news clippings: A marathon of 10km in a rural community — a fund-raising race for young people — and a winner received the prize. It was later discovered the 11-year-old boy had hidden a bicycle; halfway through the race he rode the bicycle and got ahead of the crowd, hid the bicycle again, and came in a winner.

It reminds us of the Boston Marathon when Rosie Ruiz came in the winner; yet she was not on any of the films of the race. She had ducked in somewhere and, with a burst of speed, came in the winner. These are but a reflection of the loss of moral fiber in our society.

James K. Kilpatrick, in his syndicated column, talked about this erosion of moral character at the core of our society. He surveyed 13 lawyers; one-third of them were ready to engage in perjury and encourage their clients to do the same in order to win a damage suit against a corporation.

Two coaches were indicted on charges by the NCAA of fabricating false transcripts for their athletes. At least 15 percent of the top schools are being investigated for this kind of dishonesty in the academic records for their athletes.

The University of Maryland is under investigation. Examinations are taken by *ringers*. A student pays someone to take the exam for them. On a campus with 25,000 to 30,000 students, it is very easy to slip in a ringer — for a price. A presidential candidate had such

Vol. XI May 15, 1980 No. 20

a taint on his character when, as a Harvard student, he hired someone to take his exam.

Kilpatrick puts his finger on it —this breakdown of the moral fiber of society really goes down to the breakdown of the family and the home. Parents share the blame because parents encourage their children to engage in these practices in order to compete in this kind of world. And when he puts his finger on the family and parents, he is putting his finger on the center and core of the structure of society — for the family is the basic unit of society.

THE PILLAR OF SUPPORT

Only twice in western civilization has the family completely broken down and disintegrated. The first time, the Greek city states about 300 B.C.; the second time, Rome about 300 A.D. When the structure of the family collapsed. In both cases, it brought about the collapse of society, culture, and government.

So — the crisis in our society today is not just a moral crisis; basically, it is a family crisis. That is what I want to talk about. I know a vital personal religious faith relates to the family and to marriage. Is it the key — is it the way out — is it the salvation?

I start with more evidence from the secular world. Pitirim Sorokin, sociologist of Harvard, perhaps the greatest living man in this field of relationships, made this statement from a recent survey:

Today (in 1980) one out of every three marriages end in divorce. That is a common statistic; we know this. But he went on: If there was in that marriage relationship, that family, two people who claimed to have a vital personal religious experience the divorce rate then changed from 1-3 to 1-600, an unbelievable statistic.

Furthermore: If they claim not only to have had a

126

personal religious experience, but attended church regularly, active in a local church, and had some form of daily devotional life in the family, it doubled the chances of success. Only one out of 1,129 such marriages resulted in divorce.

There is the basic thesis. The evidence is indisputable! He can stem a tide of immorality and broken family life if we will but acknowledge the part that God and religion play in family life and in marriage.

Today, there is a *universal disregard for the institution of marriage.* Sex is engaged in outside of marriage with no thought of establishing marriage or a family. It is the right of the individual to engage in this act. If I have a hunger, I have a right to get food.

So there is this materialistic, animalistic interpretation of this drive called sex that is the basic foundation of marriage and the family. All the time we see articles where the questions are raised: Is the traditional family, the traditional marriage, passe? What about just living together? What about trial marriage? We will try it for three years; if it doesn't work out, we will try another one.

What about contract marriages where you can renegotiate the marriage at a specific time? What about open marriages in which we are married but we are not committed to each other; we can get involved with someone else? Many say old-fashioned morals and ideals are passe today.

We also see an *absorption* with things instead of values.

Ye are materialistic; we are concerned about physical needs for the family, but far more than the things we need are the values: Morality, Honesty, Self-respect, Love, A sense of identity and worthwhileness for each individual in the family.

We see a breakdown of *parental authority*. Jesse Jackson, speaking not long ago in Chicago, said there is a moral breakdown in authority, discipline and development. He talked about the epidemic of failure in public schools and he puts his finger on it: Moral authority comes from parents. A child in school simply reflects the moral authority he has been taught, or the lack of moral authority in his own home.

The breakdown of the family is at the center of the social problems, especially among blacks — but among all of us. He faced it as a black leader saying, This is our real crisis.

It is a hard environment in which to build a Christian marriage. But we must come back, always, to God's ideal — his word is not silent on it. God's ideal is this:

Marriage is to be a *lifetime commitment between one man and one woman for life* — joined in a holy union — sacred — that cannot be dissolved. This true union is like two rivers that flow into one single stream; after they are joined together there is no way to separate the waters that are mixed. Or the picture we have so often at a wedding. At the end of the ceremony, the bride and groom, now married, each take a burning candle and together light the center candle and make one flame. There is no way to separate that one flame.

God in His Word says this is the ideal. There is a spiritual dynamic that puts two people together — more than one plus one equals two. It is an addition that multiplies, creating a new unity, a new union, a oneness that, together, is greater than the singleness of the two that have joined. That is what God wants for every marriage.

He wants for every child two parents, mother and father. Anything less than this is less than the ideal.

He wants for the family an atmosphere of happi-

128

ness, joy, peace, respect and trust.

These are the ideals that God has set forth. We are not at a loss to find guidance here; these traditional values for marriage and the family are not secrets. We know them — and we say we believe them! But there is such a gap between what we believe and what we are practicing today that I think the church must hold up the ideals again. Let us hold onto them. Let us magnify the ideals.

GUIDELINES FOR MARRIAGE AND FAMILY

So, I want to suggest some practical steps and practical keys for putting your marriage and your family together. The fact is there are problems.

Joyce Brothers, speaking to the American Hospital Association, said this: 4 out of 12 marriages will end in divorce — that is 1 to 3. But then, of those left, 6 of them are loveless, utilitarian relationships— marriages that are empty — marriages that hold together to protect children, to protect property, to share careers or other goals.

She affirmed that religion does make a difference. In a recent survey of prominent men in Who's Who in America, they found clergymen are most likely to have the most satisfying married lives — not that preachers are better than anyone else. The preacher as a minister is forced into a rigid kind of religious approach to life. She said, These families of clergymen combine caring, communication and responsibility with sex and, of all the professionals, are more apt to have the most satisfying marriage.

So — your faith can make a difference in your family and your marriage.

Now — the keys: First of all, wherever we are, whoever we are, whatever the circumstance might be for us, single or married, *a commitment to each other and to*

God that you are going to work at enriching your family life. You are going to work at making it go better. Marriage is a commitment, not just to love, but a commitment of fidelity. We say, I commit myself to love and to cherish till death do us part. Sometimes we cannot commit ourselves to an emotion that is hot and cold; and love is an emotion, a feeling. Sometimes that feeling runs high, sometimes it runs low; we may even doubt the existence of that feeling.

But marriage is predicated upon a moral commitment to fidelity — till death do us part. That is the Christian ideal. The emotion of love as we know it, physical attraction and love, can be destroyed. Bitterness, alcoholism and abuse, the constant put-down, or nagging can kill the emotion of love.

By the same token, that emotion can be born again. It can be developed and can grow with the opposite kind of treatment. With a deliberate thoughtful purpose I am going to act like a loving person — I am going to work at this business of making love grow. That which we thought was dead can come alive again. The Christian approach to marriage is not an emotional feeling, it is a commitment of fidelity — to be faithful, to be true, to cleave to this one and work at it and keep on working at it.

Marriage is not a 50-50 proposition; it is a 70-30 proposition, or 80-20. It is contingent upon each one of us and incumbent upon us to do 70-80 percent of what is necessary to make it go. When we approach it that way, we approach it in a way that will make it work. So, *determine you are going to stay with it* and make it go!

Then, secondly; *sit down with your family and communicate* — about the values you want to preserve — what you want your marriage to accomplish — what you want to get done in your family — goals for your children, intellectually, emotionally. Jesse Jackson

130

said the great fallacy is our values are mixed up. We will spend every night taking our children to little league ball games to practice, to help them excel as an athlete, but will not spend ten minutes a week to help them with their math.

What values do we want to nourish in our family life? What is really important — educationally— emotionally — intellectually? What spiritual values do we want to enrich in our life? God is God and He should make a difference — what difference does He make in your family? What is your attitude toward Sunday? Let's decide it. A young couple marries — is Sunday just our off day — are there values we want to preserve on Sunday? The church and our involvement in the church. What is most important — job, church, home, family? Let's get our priorities straight.

Then, a third guideline or key. *Decide how you intend to retain these values.* What routines are you going to set up? If you think religion makes a difference and you are committed to that, how are you going to practice your religion in your family? That is pretty hard to do in this mobile secular society where children are on busy schedules — the father travels — how can I preserve spiritual values?

On the farm it was a simple family life — all on the same schedule — every activity centered around the family. It was easy to open the Bible around the fire after dinner with the whole family there. It is almost an impossibility today!

But there are simple things we can do. Just the routine of grace at the table for whoever is there — a ritual, a method to give a spiritual dimension to the family. When the crises come in a family, you read the scripture and talk and pray about the problem. You pray together!

And then, fourth — *have a participating relation-*

131

ship with a church. Put your family in church. This world is full of people who say church is the last thing we do on Sunday.

The day of narrow denominationalism is over — when the halftime Baptist church and the halftime Church of Christ across the street merged — and the old Baptist deacon said. I am not going. I am against it — I have been a Baptist all my life and nobody is going to make a Christian out of me now.

Friends, this is a day in which we are not battling to save Baptists or save Christians or even Catholics. This is a battle of Christianity against the great rolling tide of the Moslem religion throughout the world, of the Buddhist religion and of atheism itself which has its hold through communism on two-thirds of the surface of this earth today. It is a time when we ought to get past our narrow denominationalism to find a church that is vital and relevant to practical daily living: I will put my family and myself in that church — I will focus on the common ground of faith, not on peripheral distinctives — I will focus on the functional practical expressions of religion. In other words, we need to look for a practical church that comes to grips with the problems we are facing in today's world.

I remember from my earlier pastorates in Kentucky — the State Convention where, session after session, we debated and fought about dancing and sororities at Georgetown College!

I say it does not make any difference to me whether you dance or not — that is not the issue these young people are facing today. I am not going to spend my time preaching one way or the other on it.

Young people today are facing a crisis of whether they are going to live together — whether they are going to move in together outside the dormitory, whom they are going to sleep with — this is the kind of moral

132

crisis facing us today!

We need a church that is ready to face the realities of this day, and to try to give some guidance to building a family and a marriage that will honor God and endure in this time of crisis.

Then, my last key: If you are grappling with a problem — your family and your marriage are in crisis — don't sit passively saying, It will work out — I will just pray about it.

My children will turn out all right. They will not turn out all right anymore so than that garden will produce strawberries and flowers if you just say, I will wait till August and then, if it has some problems I will weed it. If you are grappling with a problem in your marriage, your family, *resolve you are* going to do something about it.

Secondly, do not say, we will just turn the clock back, go back to the old days, like it used to be. You cannot turn back marriage or your family; you cannot turn back your own personality to yesterday. I will be like I used to be and everything will be all right. That is impossible! We are not the same persons today that we were yesterday. We have changed; life has changed. You cannot go back!

Third: start communicating with each other. Do not freeze up. Talk with your family. You will never solve a problem until you talk with each other. Talk to others — find some models around you. You do not have to have professional help. The best counsel for many of the problems we face is from somebody else with Christian values who worked through these same problems. Here is how we worked through it — how we came out.

As our children were growing up I found other parents who had been through it a little ahead of us.

They said, just keep your cool and do this and this. Communicate with others. Sometimes you may need professional help, both for physical problems or psychological problems. Talk about it.

And then, go from where you are. Set some goals and start moving — even if you have to go alone. I believe the real live, genuine Christian, trying every day to solve family problems and marital problems on a Christlike Christian basis, will make a difference in the family. It can influence others in that family who will start working when a real honest-to-goodness live Christian starts with a new spirit to bring new life, new values, new purposes, new goals into a marriage and into a family.

So, if God be God, believe Him. If Christ be savior, accept Him. If the church is worth having, belong to it and support it. If marriage is supposed to be Christian, then declare and determine you are going to be a Christian in that marriage. If the Christian family is the basic unit of society, determine you are going to make your family a Christian family.

The home is the foundation of all other values in life — determine that home will be yours. It has been built by your sacred and holy vows in a wedding contract. Make that home a Christian home and do something about it today.

TODAY'S CHILD, TOMORROW'S HOPE!

Prov. 22:6; Luke 1:66

In an Adult Fellowship we had as our guest, Charles Fleener, who is the Chaplain for the Jefferson County Police Force — a wonderful young man with a great testimony. He shared with us some of his experiences.

He cited this statistic that is astounding: 40% of the suicides in Jefferson County are under 18 years of age! Now, contemplate that. He said the youngest that he had had was a 10-year-old boy that hung himself a couple of years ago. He left a note that said, I have nothing to live for. Think of that — a 10-year-old boy who had nothing to live for! Something is wrong there, isn't it?

It is not natural or normal for a child not to be exuberant, happy and excited; life is always bright to a child. Somebody had to teach him there is nothing to live for. He had to live in an environment that was empty and void of values. As an impressionable baby coming into the world growing up to 10 years of age — all that surrounded him was so empty of meaningful values and content in life, that at 10 years of age, he said there is nothing to live for.

That is why I want to talk about *TODAY'S CHILDREN, TOMORROW'S HOPE!* The speaker had said the worst thing that could happen in this world would be for our children to grow up and be like us. Think about that! Was it a cranky preacher that said that? A frustrated parent? No!

This was a topnotch educator speaking to teachers

in Virginia saying again: The worst thing that could happen in this world is for our children to grow up and be like us. If there is any hope for a better tomorrow, it is dependent upon children that are better than we are, taking hold of this world — else they will have the same old world— with the same old problems — the same emptiness — the same ugliness and the same prejudices — the same sins.

We read in the papers and hear on the air of killing and stealing and crime everywhere. We sigh and say, as we notice the trend, "This young generation, where will it end?" Too much money, too much idle time, too many movies of passion and crime; Too many books not fit to be read, too much evil in what they hear said. But, kids don't make the movies, they don't write the books; they don't paint pictures of gangsters and crooks; They don't make the liquor; they don't run the bars, they don't make the laws and they don't sell the cars; they don't peddle the drugs that addle the brain — that's all done by older folks, greedy for gain. Delinquent teenagers! Oh, how we condemn the sins of the nation and blame it on them. For in so many cases, it's sad, but it's true, the title DELINQUENT fits older folks, too.

Back again — the worst thing that can happen to this world is for our children to grow up becoming just like us.

A wise man of many centuries ago gave us a challenge and a promise. In Proverbs 22:6, he gives us hope: *Train up a child in the way he should go: and when he is old, he will not depart from it.* I want us to look at that for a few minutes.

The first truth that is obvious . . .

CHILDREN CAN BE CHANGED

Children do not come into this world fixed; they can be changed. Now, the older we adults get the more fixed *we* get. But a *child is impressionable.* Here in the neighborhood someone had poured concrete for a sidewalk. I happened along a little later and saw where some child had put his footprint in that concrete; that concrete was soft and impressionable. But, let that concrete harden, and an elephant can walk on it and not leave an impression.

The point is— a child is like that wet impressionable concrete. Every experience every day leaves a mark and, as a child gets older, that print becomes fixed. So — we need to be concerned about the whole atmosphere of the family — the relationship between husband and wife, the things you talk about — if the child is exposed to bickering and hostility, sin, crudeness and wickedness at home. Those impressions will be there and harden like concrete as the child grows older.

On the other hand, if there are positive impressions, they also will harden. And the writer says they will not depart from those impressions that come in the early formative years.

I read the story of two boys who lived on a farm in the West many years ago. The younger brother idolized his elder brother. One day the elder brother became seriously ill. The father rode 20 miles into town to get the doctor. The old country doctor, in his buggy, got there about midnight. The distressed mother and father stood over the bed, so anxious as this boy was wracked by fever and convulsions. The younger brother, wide-eyed, anxious and worried also; climbed into a chair to watch all that went on.

He saw the doctor take out his stethoscope, check the boy's temperature, tap around, scratch his head — then get some medicine out of his little black bag. He saw the tenseness and anxiety on the faces of his parents — his mother was almost in tears.

137

The doctor said, Your boy is very, very sick— but we can handle it. Give him this medicine , I will check with you later. But in three weeks, he will be sound as a dollar. Don't worry. It was like a great load rolled off the backs of that father and mother; they were so relieved. And the little fellow, seeing what happened, said, I want to grow up and be able to do that for other daddies and mothers.

That one experience, that one impression, that one event in his life, shaped his destiny. He went through hardships unimaginable — odds so stacked against him that others would have said, impossible! But he worked his way through high school, and college, and into medical school until, at last, he was on the staff at Mayo Clinic, the number one physician in the field of childhood diseases. Impressionable!

If you have a child in your home — in your Sunday School class — in your neighborhood— it is possible that you may, by one experience, one time, set that child on a path that will be fixed for the rest of his life.

So — train up a child — the *child can be trained.* A child is impressionable — for good or for bad— impressionable for God — impressionable for the world.

Then we ought to be concerned about *religious education.* What kind of impression are we making on the child about God, the Bible, and prayer, about our own spiritual values? At 9:30 on Sunday morning I see the daddies drive up — in a sports shirt, not dressed for church, obviously — the children step out, all dressed up — they tell them good-bye and drive off. Maybe the golf clubs are in the back of the car — maybe they are headed to the office to work — maybe they are going back to read the newspaper. They say, I am a Christian — my life is straightened out — I just want the church to take my children and get their lives straightened out.

138

Though this may be a worthy act, to send them to Sunday School, there is an even greater impression being made that, really, church is not important. God is not important. When I get old enough, I can throw it off like my daddy or my mother — too busy — and the subconscious impression is there.

So, a child can be changed — a child is impressionable.

Well, if a child is teachable and trainable, then . . .

HOW TO DO IT

There are three obvious ways for training. The first is with *discipline*. The one sure way to bend a child. Some discipline is necessary. Our problem is that we seem to swing in extremes. Society itself swings in extremes. When I first started preaching, it was one extreme — harsh, firm, hard discipline. The authoritarian, autocratic father passed out the rules; he was rigid and absolute; there was no bending, no kindness and no loving. It was done in the name of the authority of God Himself. There was that extreme.

Then, in the ministry, I saw the pendulum swing to absolute permissiveness. A child could do anything! You were not to change them or correct them lest you warp their personality. The pendulum swung all the way over to the other extreme — according to Dr. Spock's ideas.

Now — somewhere in between, there is a middle road. Somewhere in between, there is a balance. But all of it must be undergirded by love. Let me show you what can happen, with either extreme:

A child was born into a family where the father was an alcoholic and a cobbler, a shoemaker. He would come home from work drunk and he would just, mercilessly, beat Joseph. The child had to hide to escape the beatings as this man took out his anger

139

against the world on this child. That was the extreme of brutality, rigid discipline, and harshness.

At the other extreme was an absolute doting mother. This child could do no wrong; he was a perfect child. She gave the child anything he wanted.

So this child grew up with these two extremes influencing him. And when he died — let me read what the mother said: He was always a good boy. I never had to punish him. He never did anything wrong. And who was this boy, Joseph?

Joseph Stalin — murderer of tens of millions of people without morality — head of Russia in the period of its greatest violence — who without conscience could do anything! Now, you see what it produced! A Joseph Stalin!

Now, somewhere in between permissiveness and extreme authority, we find *the center road that is the road of love.* Someone has said that if you will love a child, you can get the child to do almost anything. The secret and key to it is love. Discipline is one way we shape a child, train a child.

A second way we train a child is in *example.* The example we set. Children are born imitators. They will imitate and follow whatever we do.

Some years ago, one of the Ohio colleges gave an honorary LL.D. degree to a woman — an honorary Doctor of Law. She was a 74-year-old woman who lived at Wooster, Ohio. Her name, Ophelia Compton. She was so honored because she was a mother and because of what she had done as a mother of four children. Karl, at that time, was president of the Massachusetts Institute of Technology. Wilson was a noted attorney and economist, world-famous. The baby boy, Arthur, won the Nobel Prize in physics. The daughter, Mary, was principal of a mission school in India.

What did this mother say on that occasion?

140

Children are not likely to be any better than their parents; they will follow their example of what they do, not what they say. Doesn't that sum it up? We guide a child by discipline; by example, good or bad, and then. . .

Third, we can guide a child by *instruction*, by teaching. We are concerned about our schools. It is important for a parent to work with a child on homework, to show an interest in their studies, to be active in the PTA.

But — how interested am I in my child's religious education? Do I help my child with the homework or a Sunday school lesson? Am I interested in the projects they do in the mission class? Am I as concerned about their getting a good religious education as I am about a good secular education? When all is done, what value is making a living if you do not know how to live!

If I had it to do over again, I think I would say, I am going to have a systematic program of instruction for my children in three areas: I want to instruct them, first of all, in *the commandments of God* so they will know right from wrong. We will go over and over it — what is right and what is wrong.

Secondly, I would want to establish a pattern of *what you should believe*— we believe this and that and the other about God, about our fellowman.

Third, I would want to instruct them in *prayer* by *example* and by participation — to teach them how to pray.

Those are the three ways we can guide them. Train up a child — by discipline, by example, and by instruction.

The last obvious point here is this: We are to train up a child in . . .

141

THE WAY HE SHOULD GO

In what direction shall we train a child? I can think of three directions. Train up a child in the direction *upward,* toward God. Who are your child's heroes? What pictures are on the wall in your child's bedroom? Picture of a baseball player? That is wonderful — a good hero. Football player? Rock star? How about a picture of Jesus Christ on the wall? You help your child to find heroes in Christ Himself and in those who follow the precepts of Christ. Work on that — train up a child in this direction.

Train up a child in the direction *outward, toward others.* Teach a child to share and to love others, to see the world around them.

Then — train up a child in the direction *inward, growing inside.* Growing character. That is the greatest training. Character comes from the concepts they have about God, about others, about themselves and about life. Those attitudes form character. And the only right attitude we can get about God, about others, about ourselves, about life — the only right attitude is a *Christian attitude,* a Christian understanding of it.

In other words, the greatest thing you can do for your child is to *introduce your child to Jesus Christ. The greatest joy you can have* is to bring your child to know Jesus Christ as Saviour.

A child can become a Christian. A child is more impressionable— more ready to express faith than an adult. Children just naturally have faith. They have faith in you as a mother or father. Let me give an example:

If you were to take your child out and point to the moon, and say, See there, see that hunk out of that moon? Well, last night while you were sleeping, I climbed up there and took a bite out of that moon. What

142

would the child ask? The child would not say, How did you get up there? The child would say, How did it taste? That shows a child's faith— they are ready to believe anything you tell them.

The impressionableness of a child, the faith of a child says the child can easily become a Christian. They want to express faith — a faith in someone outside themselves, beyond themselves, greater than themselves. *A child makes the best kind of Christian.*

Who makes the best kind of ballplayer? One who started playing ball on the sandlot when he was seven years old, or one that just took up baseball at 50 years of age. Of course, the one that played from the beginning.

Who makes the best violinist, the one who started practicing at five years of age, six, eight years of age? Or one who took up the violin after they retired? Of course, the one that started as a child.

In the same way — who makes the best Christian? Those who start on the Christian life early, as a child. So I would say your child can become a Christian. Your child, as a Christian, will make the best kind of Christian the Lord and the world can have. Your child can *become a Christian easier as a child* than at any other time in life, probably. Let's try something here: How many of you came to know Jesus Christ after you were 50 years old? One or two. How many came between 35 and 50? Three or four more. How many came to know Christ between 25 and 35? A few more here. How many of you came to know Christ between 18 and 25? Quite a few more.

How many of you came to know Christ younger than 18? Look at that — many hands. How many of you came to know Christ before you were 12 years of age — keep your hand up. Not many hands went down.

Just a simple demonstration to say, Train up a

143

child in the way that he should go, and when he is old, he will not depart from it. What a promise! Right here it is.

Sow the seed in the mind and heart of your child from the time they are just a tiny baby and that seed will lie there. There may be times when you are discouraged and disheartened and you will say, What am I going to do? My child has gone as a prodigal into the far land. But, here is a promise we can hold to.

The other night we heard a wonderful testimony. A young man said, I started out on the right road. He went to the seminary, trained for the ministry — got off the track— spent some years as a nightclub singer, a professional — I enjoyed it, I have to admit. But then, 13 years ago, I came back. And he sang a beautiful song: "I have returned to the faith of my childhood."

That is the promise — for parents, and a challenge to some of us even that need to come back to the faith of our childhood, today, in a rededication.

MARRIAGE: TRIUMPH OR TRAGEDY

Matthew 19:4-6

Marriage is the most difficult of life's relationships, the most demanding, the most complicated; yet, is the most rewarding, fulfilling, promising, and offers the highest road to happiness of any human relationship.

Jesus set the ideal for marriage: From the beginning, one man for one woman for life, joined in a sacred union. I used the figure of two streams joining into one river. There is another analogy. Take hydrogen by itself and oxygen by itself — when mixed in the right proportion they produce something totally different to the former gases; they produce water. And so, literally, marriage is to be an entirely *new way of life* with depth and dimensions and meaning and significance.

But — there is a tremendous gap between the reality of marriage as we experience it and the ideal. God's desire for marriage is almost an impossible ideal, for Jesus said, *Be ye therefore perfect* . . . Yet, we are not perfect. We cannot stop living; so keep struggling toward the ideal.

I want us to look at this problem in a practical way. Out of my experience as a pastor let me share some thoughts with you.

THE CRISES

Counselors, psychologists, and psychiatrists say there are three major crisis periods in marriage. Usually if the marriage can make one hurdle, it goes well until it reaches the next one. And, significantly, these hurdles are about ten years apart.

The first hurdle is in the very first year of marriage, *the beginnings*. If the marriage lasts that first year, it has a good chance of lasting ten years or more. That first year — a couple comes together, *leaving everything* behind — mother, father, home, all relationships they have known to this point in parent-child and family relationships — *leaving to cleave to this one*. Some do not make that transition; some cannot leave; yet this is the basis of marriage, a leaving to cleave in a *new relationship to a new person*.

In Genesis we have the dramatic story where Isaac goes to Mesopotamia and falls in love with Rebekah. The question is asked of her, Wilt thou go with this man? Rebekah says, I will go. Think of this awesome decision. She was saying, I will leave everything I have ever known in life — I will leave them all to follow wherever Isaac goes.

Jesus said that is marriage. During the war, a girl marries a soldier in camp to follow him, maybe to the other side of the world. Or a theological student meets a girl; they are married; and she follows him — West, Northeast, South. Wherever God leads you, I will go, even to the mission field around the world. The businessman is transferred and the wife says, We must go wherever he as the breadwinner must go for the family's sake. This is the cleaving.

The real problem is — sometimes there is no real leaving, and then there cannot be any real cleaving. Again and again, young couples come with their problems. Some have not left home yet; they are still tied by the apron strings; still dependent upon the relationship with father and mother for their security, for their circle of friends.

Here are some guidelines for this problem. *Join a church*, first thing. You are a Christian. Quit going

146

back every Sunday, or every other Sunday. *Get in a missionary society circle — get in a Sunday School class.* Right now!

Limit your visits home to once a month. Then, make the intervals longer. If you get lonely between visits, volunteer to teach in a Sunday School class; work with Girl Scouts; do something in the social ministries— just get busy doing something!

In six weeks, if you do not know 50 people by face and by name and are able to list them, you are not really leaving and making a new life. That is a pretty good measurement.

The second crisis time is ten years later *in the middle years.* The man is forging ahead in business, the woman is busily absorbed in caring for the children and the home. The novelty of marriage has now worn off.

This is a crisis time; *they begin to look around.* The man says. I'm still young, wonder if I've really gotten all there is to marriage. Should I bail out while I have a chance to start anew? A woman, even with children, says, I'm trapped. He is absorbed in his business — gone all the time — doesn't pay any attention to the children. Am I going to have to live this way the rest of my life? She wonders about the security of her marriage. The second crisis — they get over it, though.

Then comes the third crisis: The time of *the empty nest,* the children are gone. Just the man and woman left. If they have not built a life together — if only the children have held them together; only the common interest of rearing that family — they *have nothing in* common and this is a crisis. We see this more and more, marriages of 25, 30 years. Suddenly — did you hear — they have gone on the rocks! The crisis years!

This is what the experts say — three crucial times.

147

Now this does not mean there are no crises in between, just that these times are significant.

THE CONSPIRACY

The experts also tell us there are three major conspirators, or enemies, that would destroy a marriage. They fall in these categories:

Immorality — the greatest conspirator that would destroy a marriage — the major cause. It is expressed in infidelity. We have some mistaken ideas about infidelity; it is an act, not a state and a condition.

Yet, sometimes we let a single act completely wreck a marriage, where there is no forgiveness and no acceptance, no chance of beginning again. It is all over. Somehow we need to learn that God is able to forgive. If there is sin in a marriage, it can be forgiven or overcome by the grace of God and the forgiveness of Christ in our hearts.

Drinking is another cause of immorality. From my experiences I expect drinking has been the second principal cause of breakdown. One, or both, started out with a social drink. One of them became an alcoholic. Perhaps in the looseness of the occasional party, one or the other played the fool and was entrapped in this immorality and that, in turn, sowed the seeds for the wreckage of the marriage.

The third factor is *gambling*, a greater factor than you think — the number of men and some few women, who have gotten in deep. They have borrowed money from the till and their wives knew nothing about it. They become compulsive gamblers and it wrecks the marriage.

We could put these and many other factors together to call them S-I-N, Sin! We must remember — the fact that you married does not mean Satan won't bother you any more. The temptations to sin are just as real and

148

vicious. It is not just the single person who is tempted to be immoral, but the married person also. We must constantly be on guard against Satan who would destroy the marriage by immorality.

Immaturity — the second conspirator. Emotional immaturity— one or both parties have not grown up. When Mrs. Dehoney and I married I was pastor at Rogersville in East Tennessee. Up above us was Sneedville, a backwoods mountain town, notorious because of a news story about a child mountain bride who was nine years old. I have known a lot of child brides, not a nine-year-old one though — some 19 and 29 years old, and some who are still children at 49 and have been married 25 years. I have known some grooms who have not grown up, too.

Well, why is this? We are born selfish, immature. Maturity comes to us in life as we have the opportunity. Family relationships give us the opportunity to grow out of our selfishness, but we don't do it — unless we make ourselves do it, unless circumstances force us. Indulgent parents can bring a child to maturity physically, and still have an infant child emotionally, throwing tantrums, pouting. Raise a girl; she can still be self-centered and selfish at 45. We do not grow into maturity until we are ready to do it, and make ourselves do it. It does not come automatically.

A third element that destroys marriage: *The war between men and women.* There has always been a battle: Women's lib is not new. The equal rights movement is not a cause of this generation — there has always been this struggle. Basically, the psychologists say this: Women resent men treating them as inferiors — to use as a doormat.

The man has problems, too. He is afraid of women. *Women, biologically are stronger than men.* More baby girls survive the trauma of birth.

149

Women live longer than men by about seven years. They can bear more pain. They can lose more blood, the doctors say, and still survive. Women are more emotionally stable than men. I did not think that was so until I read the statistics here. Twice as many men have breakdowns. Twice as many men go insane. Women in the long run, are more able to cope with the changing pressures of life.

Men have more heart trouble, heart disease, more ulcers. This idea of male superiority is a fallacy; men know this and they are insecure, afraid of women. So — you have warfare.

At the University of Louisville commencement Margaret Head talked on this. As an anthropologist she says, We are in a revolution. Women are discovering they are persons and are seeking fulfillment. But this revolution is entirely different from the French Revolution which was political, the Industrial Revolution which was economic. The revolution is going on in every home, everywhere. Woman is saying, Look, I have a life of my own to fulfill. I have a right to fulfillment as a person, not just a thing in marriage.

Well, those are the problems, the conspirators against marriage. We have looked at the negatives. Now, how to make your marriage triumphant, happy and abundant . . .

BUILDING BLOCKS

One is *politeness*, just sheer politeness. It is said marriage usually means the death of politeness between a man and a woman. Is that true in your marriage? It is interesting to watch a man open the door and bow and scrape to a woman he has never met and will never see again — then completely ignore the woman he has to live with the rest of his life. He ought to try to impress the right one if he wants to make points.

150

Second, *honesty.* How easily deception can come into the marriage — not about morality, but little things. Daddy does not know about the children and their problems, keep it hidden from him. A father keeps his business and financial affairs hidden, not let her in on these things. Honesty and openness with each other, no secrets between you, but sharing!

Third, *communication.* What a building block! God gave us the power to communicate one with another. No other form of life has the capacity to think, to talk and express ideas. Of all places we ought to use it, it should be in this most intimate place of marriage. There is a verse of scripture that ought to be in gold letters on the headboard of every bed in every home: Let not the sun go down on your wrath (Eph. 4:26). If there is a problem, communicate, talk it out before you sleep.

The fourth building block, *appreciation.* Four of the greatest words to bring happiness into your marriage are these, *How wonderful you are!* How long since you said that to your companion? A man could not stand up one day under the pressures of housework, of motherhood, organizing that family to keep it going and everybody on the track. The man beats his brains out in the world to bring home what his family needs. Appreciation — How wonderful you are! How long since you said that to your companion?

The final building block: *flexibility.* Life is change. Flexibility is the opposite of rigidity. We become so rigid, so fixed on one idea, on one point of view. It destroys us, and it will destroy our marriage. Every day requires adjustment to a changing world, a changing relationship.

And it is a foolish idea to think we could get 100 percent perfect adjustment in marriage. There is no such thing, because we are not perfect people. We are

151

imperfect people in an imperfect world. If you can say, We are about 60 percent adjusted — you are lucky. We have our conflicts and we are flexible so we can live with it.

A woman said, I can't stand my life any longer. What do you mean? What are you going to do about it? Unless you are prepared to commit suicide — you don't have any choice. Live with your situation and adjust to it. Quit feeling sorry for yourself and make the best of it. You can find happiness and satisfaction and peace in it.

There they are — politeness, honesty, communication, appreciation, flexibility. They sound familiar. Where do we get them?

The Apostle Paul said, The fruit of the Spirit is love, joy, peace, patience, kindness, goodness, faithfulness, gentleness, self-control. When we have had an experience with the Holy Spirit! The fruits of the Spirit are just other names for our building blocks. And those who belong to Christ have nailed their natural desires to His cross — resentment, bitterness, harshness, unkindness — nailed to the cross. If we live in the Holy Spirit's power, let us follow the Holy Spirit's leading in *every part of our lives.* In the church, in the world, in this most intimate relationship of life, marriage itself. That is Galations 5:22-26, read it.

I drove along the Florida coast after a hurricane. Some houses were swept away, only the foundation left; some were still standing. That house still standing was tied to a good foundation. Here is a good foundation but it was not tied, and the house is gone. Jesus said some are built on sand, some on a rock.

The foundation for a stable, glorious, triumphant marriage is Jesus Christ. And you are tied to Jesus Christ through the relationship in His church. You cannot go it alone; you need the strength of the church to tie you on, to help you. So when the storms of life are done, that marriage will stand.

Where are you in your marriage experience? I am still a pilgrim on mine. As the years go by, the experience becomes richer but it is still a growing experience.

Will you express a renewal of those marriage vows?

Holding you, my beloved companion, by the hand — here — in the presence of God — I give thanks to God who gave you to me and who has blessed our life together. Again I pledge to you anew those first spoken vows, that throughout sickness and health, prosperity and poverty, for better or for worse. I shall continue to love, and to cherish you.

As we walk on the pilgrim journey through the paths of kindness, and forgiveness, of understanding and of sharing together. I pledge myself anew unto you until that day when death shall separate us and bring us into the presence of our Living Lord and Savior, Jesus Christ.

HOPE FOR THE HOME

A MAN AND HIS SON

Luke 15:11-24

This is the story of the prodigal son, sometimes called the greatest story ever told. Time has not changed the characters nor the dynamics of this story. It is ageless — only the external superficialities have changed.

But — this day I want us to focus not on the prodigal himself, not even on the elder son which is the point of the story — but focus on the father and see him in all the dimensions of fatherhood at its best.

Let's imagine the setting. Perhaps it is breakfast time — the household of this farmer who has extensive lands, many flocks and two sons. While sitting at the table, the younger son speaks up and says, Father, I am of age — give me my inheritance; and the father, stunned by the request, says, Son, what is that? I want my inheritance; I want to leave home. The father with trembling heart asks himself, Is he ready — Does he have judgment — what is wrong? But then the boy speaks further, You see, I want to go out and make my own life. I live under the shadow of your name and influence here. I want to be myself! Or, I want to do my thing.

UNDERSTANDING

We see the *first measure of fatherhood* as he rises to this occasion and says to the son: I understand. He does not say I agree with the good judgment that you

Vol. VII   June 17, 1976   No.

have. He could have said you are very foolish; I don't think you are mature enough. Many things he could have said, but, he said, I understand!

He had that deep wisdom and insight to realize that there are continuing needs in this process from birth to maturity that every child must have and in fulfilling those needs, he said, I understand that now this last need you have must be fulfilled.

Here are the needs a father must provide his own as he brings this new life into the family. *The first need of that newborn babe is physical care* — for food, clothing, shelter. This is why God established a family and marriage, a sacred and holy union to preserve this place where there are two adults who will care for this little one and give him his physical needs. Most fathers do a very good job of this. But tragically, they do not go beyond this first need. They ask, What else do you want? I give you food and clothes and pay the bills!

But there are other needs — *the second need of a growing child is a sense of security* — a home, a place, a family that is a retreat and a fortress where the child may feel secure against the world — though the whole world is against me, I can come here and no one can touch me; I am secure in this one stable thing in all the world — my home, my family. The father gives that stability and security to it.

I remember an experience that I am sure some of you had when you started school. A larger boy from the third grade decided he was going to beat me up at school. Sure enough, when I came out he was waiting for me — and he did beat me up. He didn't hurt me much outside; but he hurt me a lot inside. When I picked myself up out of the dust, whipped and angry about it but knowing I could not lick him — I began to make my way toward home. When I got far enough away from him where I knew he could not catch me, I

156

turned around and shook my fist at him and said, You just wait — I'm going to tell my daddy and he'll knock your block off!

You see, I went home with a sense of security that my daddy would care for me and protect me. There was security there. He could lick anybody in the world and he could solve any problem in the world. And I say to you, It is a great tragedy that many children do not have this kind of security at home today. Where there is bickering and division, there is no sense of security and they even wonder whether there is going to be a family at home and wonder whether the daddy and mother are going to separate. I never knew that kind of insecurity and I give God thanks for wonderful parents who always gave me that great retreat of a secure and stable home.

The third need: For love and affection and concern. A father needs to give himself to his children.

Bobby Dodd, that East Tennessee ballplayer, was speaking to a group at Georgia Tech about juvenile delinquency. He said something like this: I'm no psychologist; I don't know what causes these problems in society — but as I see juvenile delinquency, I think I know the answer. I believe there are a lot of fathers who are trying to substitute dollars for daddies! In his East Tennessee way, he spoke it right. We beat our brains out trying to make money to buy things to give to our children which they do not need and, generally, will not appreciate. *What they really want is something of ourselves!*

Now there is the last need: *the progressive need for independence.* The last stage. When the boy said, Father, give me my inheritance — is that what he really wanted? He didn't want the money. He wanted to get away from home! This is natural and normal. This comes with maturing, psychologically, and

157

physically. It is time to go out and become an adult — I want to break my ties and get out and be one! Try it on my own. That is what he wanted.

Now, this can be a very unholy desire if a young person says, I want to do it just so I can be free to do as I please — just so I can be free from the restrictions and the restraints — so I can live in a wild way without the coercion of my parents.

But — on the other hand — to say I want to get away from home can be one of the finest things a young person could do. And one of the finest things a parent can do is say, Yes, I want you to get away from home. If that young person goes out to say, I want to go and be an adult, make my decisions and be responsible and take the consequences of my bad decisions and grow and be able to cope with life — dealing with it as an adult — I am ready to try to fly on my own.

You know, we as human beings are strange creatures. Of all the creatures on the earth, we alone cling and hold on to our children. The bobcat sends the youngsters out and won't let them come back and eat at the family carcass. The eagle pushes the young eaglet out of the nest and makes it fly — it is time to go and get on your own now. But we want to hold on and claim them and keep them.

This was a wise father who had this understanding. It does not mean his heart was not broken; it does not mean that he was not emotionally wracked with a great deal of anxiety and loneliness. His boy was going away. I am sure that mother had the hardest time in the world to even admit that she was willing for him to go one night away from home. But in a better understanding, she could say, I raised him to be a man; this is the only way he can be a man, to go out on his own. He was a wise father.

THE GIFT OF THE FATHER

Over the next few days, the father got the money together to give him what Deuteronomy 21:17 prescribes as the inheritance of the younger son — he got one-third of the inheritance. I see the father as he stands on the hill with the boy looking down that long road into a far country — and the scripture says, He gave unto him his living. And he gave unto him a bag of gold perhaps — here is your inheritance. But he gave him something else.

I am confident this father gave him something besides some money to get a stake in life. I think *he gave him a worthy example.* I think he put his hand in the hand of the son and said, Now, boy, I've tried to live right and set an example in front of you; I hope you remember it. He had clean hands, a clean life, and he could say to the son, I've done my best to show you how to do it right. How many fathers can say that? By the grace of God, if we have slipped and fallen and made our mistakes, God in his grace can still redeem us and redeem our lost chances — but I think this father said, I give you a good example.

I also love you, son. I've said this all along but, I want you to know that what you are doing does not break this chain of love and affection we have for you. There weren't any ultimatums issued; he didn't say, Son, there's your money, it's yours! That is the last dime you'll get. He didn't say, go your way — you're on your own — don't ever come and ask me for another thing now. I've done it for you.

He didn't say like that father who disapproved of the boy that the girl married and said, If you marry him, he's never welcome at our house! Don't ever bring him back here.

No threats, no bullying, no ultimatums, no burning the bridges over which the boy must come back if he is

159

going to be restored to fellowship with his father. It is a wise father who says, I am keeping the channels open; what you are doing is unwise; what you are doing is breaking my heart and mother's heart — I want you to know I love you; and when you get in that far country if you ever need me, you know you have a daddy at home that still cares about you. Son, you can always come back; there is always a place here for you.

How many times do I have to say, Don't issue those ultimatums. Don't explode and say this cuts this line. Keep loving, keep loving. I think that father took that boy's hand and said, I am going to keep loving you and loving you, regardless of what happens.

Then — I think he gave him a third thing: Not only a worthy example — not only love and an open door to come home, but I think *he gave him faith*. He said, Son, mother is not going to be with you, and I am not going to be with you any more; but I am going to pray that God is with you. I am going to commit you to God. Our Heavenly Father is going to be at your side; just remember that and back home mother and I are always praying for you.

It takes a pretty hard, calloused man to get away from that memory of a dad who says, Remember, mother and I have committed you to God and wherever you go in this world, you are in God's hand and we are praying for you.

I think those are some of the things he gave him besides the bag of money — and he sent him on his way.

THE FORGIVENESS OF THE FATHER

You know what happens. We are still focusing on the father. We will not spend time with the son in the far country in want, losing all that he had in riotous living, so hungry he would eat the very husks the swine would eat.

One day the son comes home — out of that desperate circumstance in a far country, coming home! Let's spotlight the father.

It says, And when he was a great way off the father saw him. What does that say to you and to me? How did it happen the father saw him a long way off? On this particular day? Time immeasurable has passed; weeks, months, years maybe. It says to me that father had gone to the top of that hill every evening and looked down that long road just to see if, maybe, today is the day the boy is coming home.

He was there watching and he saw this figure coming down the road. It looks like — It might be — It is — Yes! It's my boy coming home. The boy shouts to his father and the father shouts his recognition back to the boy; then a strange thing — he began to run — the boy began to run, but the father ran to him also. This is a very undignified thing for an oriental to do in that day. Unmanly. But it shows the compulsion of his heart to run to meet his son.

The son has his speech ready: Father, I have sinned against heaven and against thee. I think the father had a speech that he had often thought about making when he saw the son again: Where have you been? What have you been doing? Where did the money go? But, that speech is gone; the father embraces him and they kiss and weep together as the flood of the river of love flows to engulf them as the boy cries out, Forgive me, father, and the father receives him and says, Go, prepare the feast; bring out the fatted calf, the ring and the robe and put it on him. My son which was lost is found; my son which was dead is alive! Let us rejoice and be merry!

All of the dimensions of the Christian gospel are right here at this focus.

Repentance — Father, I have sinned — when we

161

say that to God, our loving Heavenly Father, the floodgates of heaven open up and His mercy and His grace begin to flow.

Repentance and forgiveness that come to cleanse us and receive us back.

The *reconciliation* — restored. Paul says we are reconciled in Christ. And here it is — a father reconciled to his son, a son reconciled to his father — that is the glory of the Christian gospel!

But the greatest of all is *justification* — look at it here. He comes back restored and made right as though he had never gone away! This is what God does for us — and the focus of the story now is not upon an earthly father, but on a Heavenly Father. And upon His invitation for us to come back.

When we come saying, I have sinned, in confession, his forgiveness flows and his grace is unbounded; His love overwhelms us and we are restored to sonship as though we had never gone away. That is the great lesson. We are focused on the father in the story — for Jesus was saying, This is the way God is; this is how He loves us. If an earthly father is capable of this kind of love, how much more is a Heavenly Father capable of this love.

Bishop Gerald Kennedy of the Methodist Church tells the story of an old Methodist circuit rider who had a wayward son. The boy was constantly running away from home and rebelling against his father. In those days, the way of the world was represented in the circus. Every time a circus came to town the boy would join up and run away with them. Every time, the father went to get him and bring him home.

One day he ran away until he found the circus in a far land and joined that circus and was living his own life as he pleased in a wild and wicked way. And his father, tracing him, and finding him, came at last and said, Son, I am here and I have come to say we love you and we want you to come home. The boy said, How in the world did you ever find me? And he said, I'll always find you because I pray to God and God tells me how to find you. It doesn't make any difference where you go, I'll always find you.

Bishop Kennedy said the boy dropped his head, overwhelmed by such persistent love, and said, I am coming home. And I am coming home to stay, Dad. And Bishop Kennedy says, He not only came home to the father physically, but he came home to God, and surrendered his life to the ministry and he is now one of our great ministers in one of the great Methodist churches.

That is the story of God's love — pursuing us wherever we are — into the farthest country — and calling us to come home.

HOPE FOR THE HOME

COPING WITH CONFLICT IN MARRIAGE

Ephesians 4:26-32

Read the scripture from the New International Version:

In your anger do not sin: Do not let the sun go down while you are still angry, and do not give the devil a foothold. v. 26

Do not let any unwholesome talk come out of your mouths, but only what is helpful for building others up according to their needs, that it may benefit those who listen. And do not grieve the Holy Spirit of God with whom you were sealed for the day of redemption. Get rid of all bitterness, rage and anger, brawling and slander, along with every form of malice. Be kind and compassionate to one another, forgiving each other, just as in Christ God forgave you. (vs. 29-32)

A young married couple, with a fine Christian heritage, established what they called a Christian home and a Christian marriage. However, they soon found their personalities were quite different. Two people, who come into marriage, each brings with them different concepts, backgrounds and all the baggage of their previous years of emotional experiences in the household in which they lived. It soon became apparent that he was a quiet sort of person; in fact, he had a tendency to keep everything bottled up inside him. He sulked and pouted — and then he told his mother about the problems they were having in marriage.

Vol. X May 31, 1979 No. 22

It soon became apparent that she was the explosive kind of person. She just let it loose and let it fly whenever she wanted to and she said some pretty harsh things when she did it.

So it was that one Sunday morning — they both taught their Sunday school classes, and then sat together in church. On the way home they got into an argument.

By the time they sat down for dinner, it was a full-fledged fight. She said some very sharp things to him. He jumped up from the table, ran up to his room, threw himself on the bed and pouted. Awhile later she marched into the room and said, Have you called your mama and told her about the fight? With that she ran into another bedroom, closed the door and locked it.

He bounced off the bed, angry as could be and finally exploded all that had been bottled up. He ran to the locked door — and he beat the door down. He had her by the neck and was shaking her before he finally got hold of himself. Sunday school teachers — Christians — church members — went to church — taught Sunday school. What am I trying to say?

I am saying there are a couple of myths we need to dispel immediately. Number one — if you are a Christian you never get angry. Why — you — a Christian? What are you doing getting mad? Where did we ever get the idea that a Christian will not get mad? Jesus, Himself, became angry. He said some very harsh things to the scribes and Pharisees. Now Jesus never became angry toward people who did something to Him; but He did become angry with people for what they were doing to each other. There is a vast difference.

There are some things we ought to get angry about — moral principles. The wrath of God — the anger of God — is God's defense against injustice. Paul said, Be angry — go ahead, be angry — but sin not. Do not let it lead to sin.

A second idea that is a myth: When two Christians — if they have a Christian marriage — they never fight; they will never be angry with each other. Now, that is not so; that is a myth. There are conflicts in marriage. I want us to talk about those conflicts in marriage and how to cope with them.

MARRIAGE IS ADJUSTMENT

Here is the sequence. First of all, two independent personalities begin to try to blend together two different lives. Immediately, there are conflicts because there are decisions that have to be made, choices to be made. Two people, instead of one, have to decide what to do, and, as decisions are faced, there is conflict and soon, frustration. There comes a struggle for supremacy, and then comes anger. And these follow as surely as day follows night.

The decisions they face may involve many things. First is an environmental decision. Where are you going to live? What are you going to live in? An apartment? Buy a house? How are you going to spend your money? House or car?

Then there are decisions to face also about values and goals and priorities. What is important in life? What do we put first?

Finally, there are decisions involving personality adjustments. Different kinds of personalities trying to get along together. One example of this: Someone has called it the conflict between the larks and the owls.

A lark is a bird that is ready with the dawn. With the first rays of the sun, the lark is up and greets the day: This is the day the Lord hath made — get up — let's go!

Then when the sun goes down and it is dark the lark is ready to go to bed. That is the lark's way of life

167

— that is the nature of the lark.

But then, there is the owl. When morning comes, the owl says, What's good about a day that begins with morning? I don't even believe in God before ten o'clock in the morning. But when the sun goes down, the owl is coming alive; the later it gets the better the owl is at doing and thinking and acting.

Now — what happens when a lark marries an owl? There is conflict. There is frustration. Then, there is anger.

Now, it is interesting to see how specialists in this field analyze what causes conflicts. This is a survey made among Christians — among church members. It would not be valid for the population as a whole, but it is enlightening to us as church members and Christians.

They found that 37% of the couples said the one greatest problem they had was financial — conflict over how they spent their money. Number one problem! Next came the discipline of the children — father too lenient, or too harsh — mother does not discipline or does too much.

Third, recreation and leisure. And way down the list, number eight, was sexual adjustments and physical problems. That was an amazing insight. Apparently in this day, we have a better understanding of the physical, sexual relations and how to adjust to conflicts there than we have of these other issues.

I spoke with a young couple in the vestibule. I asked, How long have you been married? Three years. Do you ever fight? Yes, we do. I said, Flossie, do you ever get so mad you wish you could stomp him? I sure do. All right. We get angry!

Now the question is . . .

168

HOW TO HANDLE OUR ANGER

We have to handle it; we had better learn how to handle it. The child that does not learn how to handle anger is in trouble.

The door will not open; the child kicks the door. And you spank him and say, You cannot get mad at the door like that.

Or a two-year-old eating at the table decides he does not like the food and dumps it on the floor. That is bad — you cannot let your anger loose like that, and you begin to spank. We know that if we do not teach a child to handle his anger, the world will make him handle his anger — or teach him some hard lessons.

Last week a man was executed in Florida in the electric chair. Regardless of your position on capital punishment, let us recognize this — society says to people, if you cannot handle your anger, we cannot let you explode and vent your anger in any way you feel. You killed a man in anger, your companion there, and we are going to make you pay for it. So — we have got to learn how to get hold of our anger.

Jesus had something to say about anger. In the Sermon on the Mount, Jesus said, Ye have heard that it is said, Thou shalt not kill . . . but I say unto you, whosoever is angry with his brother without cause is in danger of the judgment. What did he mean?

He meant exactly what He said. Anger is a dangerous emotion. If we do not handle it and cope with it in any relationship in life, we are liable to get into a situation where God will pronounce judgment upon us for what we do. And Paul was saying here in the New English translation:

When you get angry, do not let your anger lead you into sin. Do not leave a loophole for the devil to get in — because that is where the devil gets in.

169

So — how do we handle our anger in our marriage — when we have conflicts? Let's lay down some principles that will help us in every conflict. In conflict there is anger; if we can handle the anger, it will help us handle the conflict.

First of all, *let's be honest about our anger.* Do not say, I'm so hurt. You are not hurt; you are mad! Do not go around being pious — I'm such a good Christian. Be angry! I'm mad! Say it. Be honest about it. Don't sulk and hold it in.

Little children are this way. They get angry. A child says, I'm so mad — I'm going to kill you! The mother grabs the child up and runs to the pediatrician and says, What am I going to do with this little monster? He says he is going to kill his little brother! Don't worry about that — he is just being honest. The child has not learned to be a hypocrite yet and cover up that anger.

So, especially in the most intimate relationship of marriage — we need to be honest! Look, I'm angry — I'm upset about this. Be honest and open about it.

Secondly, we need to understand why we are angry — why I am angry or why somebody else is angry. Why are we angry? Things start out as just a little tiny frivolous issue — and suddenly, it escalates until it explodes in a big fight and both are angry.

Now, what causes this sequence? Psychologists say the first cause, and major cause of anger is frustration. Here is an ant crawling across the pulpit. I put my finger in front of that little ant, it turns. I put my finger there and it turns again — I put my finger there and it turns — again and again. In a few minutes, that ant, theoretically, ought to become psychotic. That ant will become frustrated. Then that ant will get mad and will bite me. I am frustrating it. It is trying to go somewhere and I am blocking it. So — we are frustrated

170

and we become angry.

A man goes to his job — he wants to get ahead — he works hard — but some unfair manipulation gets somebody else ahead of him and he does not get his promotion. He is frustrated, but be cannot punch his boss in the nose; he would lose his job. So — he comes home and takes it out on his wife.

Then she, not as strong as he, does not fight back with him; she spanks the kids. She is frustrated; she did not do anything to him; it happened at the office. The children cannot respond to their mother whipping them so they kick the dog.

Now that is the sequence. Just apply that. We are frustrated. Analyze your anger and analyze the other person's anger. That is why I am angry. I am trying to do something and it seems I get frustrated. That is why I am upset. Then you can work on that, rather than being angry about it.

A second cause — people get angry because *folks try to dominate them.* That makes us all angry — we all want to protect our self-esteem. When somebody else makes us feel little and pushes us down — even if it is a mate that does it — we get angry. We may express that anger or we may just sullenly hold it in and say, I'll get even with you.

We do this in many ways. Unfortunately, some people try to use the scripture to dominate others. One woman said, I have heard the Apostle Paul quoted so many times by my husband that when I get to heaven, if I see the Apostle Paul, I'm going to try to trip him. Paul says, Women, be in subjection to your husbands. Every time anything happened in the household, the man would say, Paul says be in subjection — I have domination over you. You are to obey me.

That is not consistent with the scripture. God did not intend for anybody to be put down like that. There

171

are roles we have to play in life — a woman's role and a man's role — but as far as identity is concerned, everyone of us ought to feel that we are somebody and we are important in the sight of God, and in the sight of those who love us.

Women try to dominate husbands and put them down and make them feel just like they are slaves to them and they must knuckle under to them.

A good marriage is made of two people who love each other too much to want to dominate the other. A man who really loves his wife does not want to make her feel like she is second rate. A woman that really loves her husband does not want to make him feel like he is a heel and abuse him. We get angry when people put us down.

A third cause: He get angry because *of revenge.* Trying to get even. When you have a fight going, it is just to get back. You did this — and I'll get back. When I was a boy we used to play catch, throwing the ball back and forth. Then we would play burn-out. You start slow and easy, then throw to the other person harder and harder until one knocks the other one out — they cannot catch it — it is so hot. I see that between husbands and wives all the time. Burn-out. I am going to give more back to you than you gave to me — I'll get even with you.

HELPS IN HANDLING ANGER

Then, I have five helps for you in handling your anger.

Number one — when you are dealing with your anger and your conflicts, *attack the act and not the person.* Do not say, You're such a lowdown husband — anybody that would do that. Rather say, What you did was not good — I didn't like what you did — the act — it bothers me — it makes me mad. Now, I think you are a wonderful

172

person. Do not attack the person's identity; attack their act.

Then *secondly, forget past mistakes.* Put them behind you. If you are going to have a right relationship with anyone — in marriage or any other relationship — forget the past. A man said, Every time I get in a fight with my wife she gets historical—she brings up everything I have ever done.

Number three. Keep your fighting up-to-date. Do not let it pile up. Some people have a gunny-sack approach. Every time the other person upsets them, they just silently put that anger in the bag. Pretty soon, they get the bag full of angers and hostilities and it explodes. It is very destructive. You need to keep it up-to-date — you need to work on it every day.

Paul said, Let not the sun go down on your wrath. Do not let the day come and pass without your saying, Let's settle this — let's don't carry it through the night.

Then, fourth, forgive. Here is the key. Be generous one to another, tender-hearted, forgiving one another as God in Christ forgave you. That really puts it in a different plane. If God has forgiven me of my sins, and He is not angry with me — then how much more must I forgive you.

Then, fifth, pray about it. I am convinced that none of us can handle our anger by ourselves — you cannot do it in your own human resources. In spite of all the logic I present — that this seems sensible and logical and psychologically sound — and all the scientists and psychologists can tell you— this is right — you say, I cannot do it. You discover that you have anger, you have conflict, things explode and you can never patch them up. The reason? We are not capable!

Paul said, That is the pagan's problem— their hearts are hard because of sin. But you have become a new creation in Christ Jesus. Only by the power of

173

God working in us through a personal faith in Jesus Christ — a personal presence of Christ, day by day — can you reach out and take the one you love by the hand — to touch them—did you ever try to fight by holding hands! It is pretty hard to fight and be angry touching them.

You see, the closer we are in love, the more healing power there is. When we have conflicts and can touch and love and, in Christ, find a common ground praying together, and forgive each other — you build a stronger relationship, each with the other, and both with God.

That is the answer — not just in marriage — but in every human relationship. Jesus Christ is the key. If you do not have Him in your heart, you are not equipped to handle the conflicts of life that come to you.

Will you take Jesus Christ into your heart as your Savior, today?

THE KEY TO A HAPPY HOME

Ephesians 4:29

If I were to give out a questionnaire this morning to ask your opinion on the most common cause of unhappiness in marriage and in the family, what would you say? Some of us would mark overt sins, alcoholism or unfaithfulness, maladjustments, stress in the marital relationship and physical relationships.

But, do you know what psychologists and counselors tell us? It is summed up in one word — *communication*. We never talk to each other. The woman says, I have been married 25 years and I feel like I am married to a stranger — he just sits there in front of that television like Old Stoneface — all I ever hear from him are grunts. He says, She talks all the time — she was vaccinated with a phonograph needle, I think. But we never talk about anything; she just goes on and on and that is it!

Or they say, When we do try to talk about things, you always blow up — you cannot be calm — never rational — too emotional — and on the blame-laying goes.

Now you say, I am not married — this sermon will not apply to me. Yes, it will, because communication is also the number one cause of unhappiness in the whole family setting — between parents and children — brothers and sisters, and so on. The children say, My parents never really listen to me. They never really heard what I was trying to say — they did not think I ever had any good ideas. Even this week a parent said, I cannot get through to my teenager!

Communication is more than just conversation. It is the whole relationship expressed by dress, by actions, by gestures, even the look on the face — the tight-lipped "yes" of a mother indicating disapproval and irritation. The father reads the paper and says, Uh-huh, go ahead.

We communicate by our dress. The judge wears a robe, and that communicates something. The policeman in uniform communicates a very clear signal to everybody. A nurse in her white uniform communicates without saying a word. Even teenagers wearing long hair and torn jeans show their rebellion against the accepted patterns. I want to set my own patterns.

Dr. John Drakeford, an outstanding man in marriage counseling, says the single most important factor for building a good marriage is good communication. So — why don't we communicate? I picked up an intriguing paperback by John Powell: *Why I Am Afraid to Tell You Who I Am*. This book sets forth some new concepts about communication.

He, first of all, lists *levels of communication*. We are always communicating; but we communicate at different levels. People move from the lowest level to the highest level; and only when you get to the highest level of communication do you really begin to live.

But the lowest level: *the cliché communication*. We have a happy word for everybody, but it is just a cliché. How are you today? If that person stops to tell us all their aches and pains, we back out quickly. Do not ever ask so-and-so how they feel or you are there for ten minutes!

We all want to be good conversationalists but we want to keep the conversation at this cliché level. I heard a story that illustrates this. This fellow had been invited to a banquet and was to sit at the head table. He said, When I get with prominent and important people,

I do not know how to carry on a conversation. His friend said, Just ask the right questions to get the conversation going and the other person will think you are a fine conversationalist.

The questions: Are you married? — where did you meet? — and they will tell all about themselves. Another good question is: Do you have any children? Ask their names, ages — where they are in school — if one is married — any grandchildren? That is good for a long time.

So, the man went to this elite banquet and was seated beside this elegant lady. After the food was served, he thought he would start — Do you have any children? Yes, I have five — tell me about them — and so on. He thought again and asked, Are you married? And that was the end of the conversation.

We all have these clichés that get us started, and we think we are talking to people. But we are not really communicating. So, that is the lowest level.

The next level: *We report the facts and opinions of others*. This we commonly call gossip. I heard so-and-so bought a new house — wonder how much they paid for it — I saw it in the paper — wonder where he got the money — I heard so-and-so was going with so-and-so — why did they break up?

Or reporting facts: Did you hear, so-and-so said to so-and-so? We are very safe with this; we do not have to reveal anything. We do not reveal our approval or disapproval. We do not say that is bad or that is good. We just keep talking as we report the facts of what people said or what they did. The great mass of people never get above *cliché* or just *reporting the fact*.

The next level: where you really start communicating is when a person begins to *share my ideas, my judgment, my thoughts*. I begin to open up and reveal me — this is what I think — this is what I believe. I am

177

not afraid to let you see into me. You might approve or disapprove. Nevertheless, *communication is revealing and sharing feelings.* Even so, you have just begun to communicate when you say, This is my idea — my judgment — my thinking.

The highest level is when you can finally say, This is how *I feel* about it — these are *my emotions.* Communication is the kind of openness and honesty and trustworthiness where people can be truthful about their emotions and their feelings — whether it is husband and wife, parent and child, brother and sister. I know it is not good, but I am honest enough to tell you how I feel — angry — hurt — happy. I feel uncomfortable, and here is why — here are my feelings — knowing they can trust the other person to look at those feelings without condemnation or rejection.

So — the question is: *How do you feel down deep in your heart?* How do you feel about yourself? Do you dare to let anybody else know or even look at yourself? Can you be that honest? How do you really feel about the person you married? What would happen if you opened your heart to say, This is really how I feel about our marriage. Powell says that is communicating — when you get to that level. That is our goal this morning. Now — *HOW* can you communicate?

The Apostle Paul was talking about this in the scripture. This letter we call *Ephesians* is considered by many to be the greatest of Paul's letters. Paul always lays down theological concepts; then he moves into the practical application.

In the first three chapters, Paul deals with theological foundation. He talks about *our redemption* — how God redeemed us — it was from the foundation of the world in the heart of God. Before the creation of the world, God purposed in his heart to redeem us, and he provided for that redemption when he sent Jesus

178

Christ to redeem us.

In chapter four he talks about *the Christian's walk* — the way he lives — and *the Christian's talk* — his conversation — his communication. In chapter five he wraps it up with a practical application of how a husband and wife are to relate to each other on the basis of God's redemption and a Christian's walk and a Christian's talk. And Paul uses the very word that is so popular today, *communication.*

Now, why don't we communicate? What are *the blocks to communicating*? I think I can sum it up with two basic blocks.

First of all is the *block of fear*. We are afraid to open up and show our emotions. One of the most penetrating writers of our day, Victor Frankl, in his book, *Man's Search For Meaning,* relates a personal experience. Now this man is a Jew who was in the concentration camp at Dachau during World War II. There were fellow prisoners in the darkness of that camp that just lived from moment to moment. They longed to escape — they longed for the day when they could get the fresh air and sunshine.

The time came and the doors of the prison opened. They came out, blinked their eyes in the sunshine, looked around and then, terror filled their faces. They were afraid. And they walked back into the darkness. They had been in prison so long they were afraid to be free. And that is the problem with many of us. We are afraid to be open and honest. Why?

Why am I afraid to let you know how I really feel? You will not like me. I do not like myself, so I know you will not like me. You will reject me — make fun of me. Or you might not even care — that would be the worst of all. In order to establish communication we have to be open and honest in a two-way experience to be able to say — this is the way I feel and I know you will keep on loving me; you understand and you do care.

And then, the second block: perhaps the block that is the most difficult to deal with — *the block of resentment and bitterness*. Paul deals with that specifically as he uses the words, anger, malice, hatred, bitterness. We resent what the other person has done to us. This is like a briar in your thumb. There is nothing more painful because your fingers are so sensitive — so many nerve endings are there. The briar is deep. You let it stay there; it gets infected and it festers and that hurts even more. After all the pain, the festering and the infection, a callous forms around it and nature takes care of it. It gets hard and tough; It is almost like a gravel in your thumb. And that is what happens when we keep resentments, hurts, and anger bottled up inside us. It poisons us; we get hard; we do not feel anything any more.

Resentments come from anger, they tell us. And a part of our problem is that we have not learned how to handle our anger. I will have to admit that, through the years, I have had the basic idea that it is wrong to get angry. A good Christian does not get angry. But that is not so — either psychologically or scripturally.

The Apostle Paul says, Be ye angry — go ahead, be angry, Be ye angry and sin not. The emotion of anger is human, and natural, normal. Anger stems from frustrations, and there is not a person in this world that does not get frustrated at some time. Take that 7-month-old grandson of mine — I restrained him and he got frustrated, he wanted to roll over. Then he was angry — frustrated and then angered. A man on his job is trying to reach an objective when somebody gets in his way and blocks him. He gets frustrated, then he gets angry. The wife wants her husband to listen while she talks about needing a new washing machine. He will not put the paper down — pretty soon she gets frustrated and then she gets angry!

We have to learn how to handle our anger as Christians, so it does not lead into sin. It is like a triangle: Emotion is the base; it is neither good nor bad; it does not make us good or bad. One person gets angry, another does not; that does not mean one is better than the other.

It is what they do with that anger — how the intellect and the will deal with the emotion. The intellect and will are the two sides, and emotions is the base. If my anger makes me punch you in the nose and knock you down, I have converted my anger into sin and violence. But if my anger says I surely *feel* like knocking you down — you made me so mad I want to knock you down — but that is the way *I feel* about it. Now, let's talk about it. I have gotten it off my chest — I have let my intellect and will control it so I can rationally face it and let you forgive me, as I ask for your forgiveness for getting angry about it. Now that is a marvelous insight from John Powell as to how to handle your emotions.

Paul says, Be ye angry and sin not. Go ahead — but do not sin in it! Have the kind of communication you can relate to the ones you love. Paul also says, Let not the sun go down upon your wrath — same idea. Your wrath builds up from the frustrations of the day — but do not let the sun go down on it. Do not let it stay there and fester.

What happens if you do not get it out? If you do not blow up in a loving accepting situation and communicate your emotions — what do you do? You clam up — you close up — you suppress it. Jay Adams, a Christian psychologist, told of a counseling situation he had with Sue and Wilbur.

Wilbur came in and slumped into a chair — you could tell he was the one in trouble. Sue came in, confident, and immediately took the conversation. I am not here because I wanted to come here! My doctor said I had to come because this man is killing me, pointing to Wilbur as he slumped a little lower. I have ulcers and they are killing me, and my doctor says he is the cause.

With that she opened a suitcase-size purse and flipped onto his desk a manuscript an inch thick and typewritten on both sides of the paper. That's what is killing me right there. It was a day by day account of everything Wilbur had done to her for 14 years. And, later counseling proved it was a pretty accurate report.

He looked at Sue and said, In all my years of counseling I have never seen a situation like this or met anyone like you. Sue grinned and Wilbur sank a little lower. I have never met a person as bitter and resentful as you are, and Wilbur sat a little straighter. This book is not only a record of Wilbur's faults and how his faults hurt you — and I know they did —it is also a record of your sin against him, and against God, and your sin against yourself for which you are now paying. And he was right! Her resentment and bitterness were killing her, not Wilbur.

All of us carry a notebook, not a physical notebook, just a mental notebook. How often we say, You always do — you have been keeping a record — why do you *always* react like that — you *never* do — you never tell me — never say that — never do this. That means you have been keeping a record. If we build up resentments and catalogue them, they will poison us.

Paul brings us to a perfect conclusion. The answer is *forgiveness* — he uses the word grace. Nothing is more defeating than legalism. Nothing can destroy a relationship quicker than the attitude of an eye for an eye. You did this to me — I am going to do that to you. No one is perfect. Everybody makes mistakes — everybody messes things up — children, adults, teenagers break things — men, women fail and forget — all goof off sooner or later — some more than others — none are perfect. Anyone expecting perfection of themselves or of someone else will impart a lot of misery and unhappiness. We must realize our human weakness. All of us will sin — not just make mistakes, but will commit grievous sins sometimes. Nobody is perfect.

We had a death in our church family this last week. His name was John Mays. He was the crippled man who lived at Keeling. He was so bent over and so drawn he was barely able to walk. What if I had said, John, straighten up, don't walk that way. You would have quickly said, That is the most unkind human being I have ever seen — to say to that poor cripple to quit walking that way.

And yet, we are all crippled. It is not as obvious, but we are all crippled by sin. And it is just as unkind to say to a wife, Straighten up — what did you do that for? Or to a husband, Why did you do that? Or to a child. . .

The grace of God is working with all of us who are crippled emotionally, crippled spiritually, crippled by sin. God is trying to help us walk a little straighter.

But for us to pass judgment and condemnation upon someone else who is less than perfect is not being Christian.

Paul says, Be tender hearted, *forgiving* one another, even as *God has forgiven* us for Christ's sake.

If God has forgiven me through Jesus Christ, then I am able to be forgiving toward someone else. Yes, even a wife, a husband, a child, a parent in the family.

Forgiveness is the ultimate key that opens the door to honest communication where we can trust each other enough to say, This is how I really feel.

And when we can express our feelings and not

bottle them up, we begin to understand what real grace and love is, one for another.

WHAT MAKES A HOME CHRISTIAN

Colossians 3:12-21

The newspaper article is headlined. Marriage is a quiet hell for half of American couples, according to a survey conducted by Dr. Joyce Brothers, syndicated columnist and psychologist who is very popular as a writer, particularly on marriage and marital problems.

Speaking before a convention of the American Hospital Association this week she said four of *every twelve* marriages are likely to end in divorce, while another six become loveless "utilitarian" relationships to protect children, property, shared careers and other goals. Not a very pretty picture of the family scene in America. It is a far cry from what we read a moment ago in the scriptures as Paul said, Husbands, wives, children, here is how you should live together.

Dr. Brothers makes some interesting observations. In the surveys she has made, women are stronger than men in life and death crises. Wives start most of the fights between spouses. Women complain more about their marriage than men. Married women complain most about money, about their husbands' drinking and about physical abuse; while men complain almost exclusively about sex.

In surveys of prominent people from *Who's Who in America* it seems that clergymen are most likely to have satisfied married lives. They combine caring, communication and responsibility with sex, she says. That does not mean that preachers are any better than anyone else. It does not mean that they are super

Vol. XV May 10, 1984 No. 19

human; they are just as human as any other man or woman. Their marriages have the same kinds of tensions, the same kinds of problems, the same kinds of adjustments.

I think there is an explanation of why Christian clergymen have been able to achieve the best kind of marriage relationship and family relationship. First of all, there is the external pressure on the part of society. Society looks at the minister and his wife and says — We expect you to make it go. If you do not make it go, who can? You are the teacher of Christian principles. You are the one to set the example of what a Christian ought to be. There is an external pressure that many ministers and their wives find difficult to live under — it is a superhuman expectation. Nevertheless, society says you have to stick with it and make it go. Would to God there could be this kind of pressure on every one of us as Christians to say, It is our Christian moral responsibility — our example to a lost world.

And what is it we do to make a marriage Christian — as Paul describes? What really makes a marriage Christian? We usually say membership in a church— going to Sunday School — living by the Ten Commandments — tithing. I will have to say that I have dealt with a lot of marriages that have been on the rocks, or went on the rocks, and they checked out on every one of these items. It is really not a legalistic listing of things to do that makes a marriage and a family Christian.

It is more *an atmosphere.* It is more a feeling that is in the family that makes it Christian — even like a church. When you walk into a church, you feel an atmosphere in that church — by the music they sing — by the way people speak in the church — an atmosphere created by the person sitting next to you. You either feel it is cold — indifferent — ritualistic and uncomfortable

186

and you are not sure you are wanted — or you feel this is a happy place — people are rejoicing —their music is uplifting — it has an up beat. People are friendly. They hand you a songbook— they speak— they care. It is an atmosphere. That is exactly what Paul was saying in the scripture we read. It is Christian living by those in the home that makes it Christian.

Now — if there is any place where we ought to be living like Christians, it ought to be in the home. But — it is a strange thing. We are so polite at the office — so Christian in dealing with that little waitress when she brings the food — say such nice things to her and even give her a Christian tract. Then — we come home and live like the devil with our wives and our children. I have seen it again and again. Home is the first place where we ought to be Christians.

That is what Paul says. He spins off these characteristics of how a Christian ought to live. And he says, Live these Christian standards right there in your home with your wife, with your husband, with your children, with your parents.

Let's pick up some of these words — not all of them — just the ones that stand out in big bold letters, ten feet tall, and maybe they encompass some of the others.

The first word, above all is *love*. *Love characterizes a Christian family*. The home is the center of the Christian faith. Someone says, We have a Buddhist home — or we have a Jewish home — or we have a Moslem home. If you go back to their religion, what is the key word in their religion? In the Jewish religion, the key word is *law* — the law of the Lord. Then you go to the Buddhist religion and the key word is *truth* — enlightenment. In the Moslem religion, the key word is *will* — the will of Allah. It is predestination — it is God— God predetermines everything.

But in the Christian faith, the central word is *love*.

God so loved the world, that He gave His Son, who so *loved* us, that He gave His life to die for us. Love! So I would have to say, if you are going to be a Christian, you are going to love, first of all. You are going to love in the home and in the family. What does that mean? I am not talking about the kind of Hollywood love where you say, I looked and I saw — the bells rang and the skyrockets went off and I knew I was in love with you. And the next day — I am ready to marry you— because I fell head over heels in love with you! That is infatuation, but that is not love. That is sexual and physical attraction, but that is not love. Love is something much deeper than that.

Love is acceptance. Love is accepting a person as that person is, and loving them as they are. Love is not trying to make them over — to change them — always to force them into the mold you want them to be. Just love them as they are.

Even with our children, that means we do not expect a four-year-old to act like an eight-year-old. Or we do not demand of an eight-year-old that they be as mature as a 15-year-old. Or we do not look to a 15-year-old to say, You ought to be grown and mature and responsible in what you are doing, like a 25-year-old. We have to accept them as they are and love them as they are.

Love is the assurance that you are going to care about a person regardless of what they do— regardless of what they are. Love is acceptance— love is caring.

Love is communication — communicating with the other one and liking to communicate. Even if you do not say anything, just being together is communication — just sitting in the same room together.

Last Wednesday in our Bible study, Dr. Songer told this story about a couple. They were in conflict. He did something she did not like and he would not do what she wanted him to do. She just said, Well, I'll just give him the silent treatment for about three days — that will bring him around! Of course, Dr. Songer said that would be a blessing to some husbands instead of a curse. But — that is no way to act in a marriage.

So — what makes a home Christian? It is where there is love — more than just a sexual attraction that soon physically exhausts itself and is spent. Love goes on and on above and beyond that.

I see another word that stands out in bold face type. The word is joy — singing. I use the word, joy, but it is *singing songs with grace in your heart*. It is joy! It is a Christian home where there is joy— where people are happy — rejoicing. As Paul says, Rejoice in the Lord; I say unto you again, Rejoice, rejoice! He kept saying that all the time, even when he was in prison — when he was suffering. Rejoice!

That is a characteristic of a Christian. Not complaining — not sour on life. What is wrong in Washington? What is wrong at the office? All the crooks are around — these sorry neighbors I have — those people down at the church — griping — bellyaching — complaining — down on the world. That is not Christian. That is not a Christian outlook on life. That is not a Christian relationship with the world as it is. Rejoicing, Paul said. Singing songs, he said. Joy in a home! Joy!

I talked with a family that was having trouble. The wife said, He is just like a sergeant in the Army. When we come to the table he says. Sit down — sit down — Sit down — you there, you there, you there— sit down and let's eat. I don't want any foolishness here at the table. We just sit there trembling. The children are just terrified. And before it is over, regardless of what we try to do at the table or how we try to have some kind of family communication, he gets mad and sends one of the children from the table It never fails —for one reason or another — Leave the table! Go to your room! Little wonder that marriage went on the rocks. Who could live with a man like that? So, you see, no joy.

When the family is together — eating together — that is the time when there ought to be warmth, happiness and joy. The Lord ate with his disciples in the most sacred hour of His life. They ate together and they sang a song and went out. Somebody asked Zig Ziglar, the motivational speaker, Did Jesus ever laugh? And he says, As far as I know, nothing in scripture ever says that Jesus laughed. But —when I was converted and saved, He sure fixed me so I could laugh. The joy of the Christian life.

I see another word here that needs to be translated *tenderness* — compassion. Bowels of mercies — that is tenderness. Jesus took the little children in his arms— that is tenderness. He held them to Himself — that is tender caring.

The psychologists tell us that is one of the problems we have today in bottle-feeding babies. It is so easy to give the baby a bottle and put it to bed. That baby needs to be held and hugged while being fed. That is why there is a tendency to go back to natural feeding. Psychologically, we need the tenderness of touching. Notice how many times Jesus reached out and touched someone — the leper — the blind man — touching — touching — touching. That is tenderness.

Yet, this is a world that lacks it. Instead of tenderness we have abuse. Instead of laying a hand in kindness and tenderness, we lay a fist with brutality upon a little child. Child abuse! I read where this man swung his little three-year-old child around the room and broke a bone in the child's arm. When the child kept crying, he took the child to a tub of hot water and submerged that child to make it quit screaming and

190

crying. When the baby came to the hospital, it was near unto death — and did die. The man was charged with murder and convicted. As far as I am concerned, he ought to be buried under the jail for that kind of brutality. Instead of tenderness — warping — twisting — breaking — destroying.

There is psychological abuse also, instead of tenderness. Child abuse all around us, psychologically. In a restaurant not long ago, there was a man with a couple of children — the smallest, a boy about four years old. He knocked over his glass of milk and the father went into a rage. You stumbling fool — you idiot — can't you ever do anything right? You always make a mess of everything — now sit up there— quit your crying and sit there or I am going to paddle you good. He abused the child verbally.

What kind of man will that little boy be when he has been beaten down all his days by his daddy who says, You are stupid— you have two left hands — you stumble — what is the matter with you — can't you ever do anything right?

And there is spouse abuse. It is appalling to me to think that a man would draw back his fist and strike a woman across the face. I just cannot comprehend that kind of physical abuse. But — I see psychological abuse all the time — not with the fists but with words. A man was beating his wife when he said to me, I am married to the ugliest woman that ever lived. I have never seen anybody like her. Fat slob — who could love anybody like that? No wonder she left him. That is abuse that no wife should tolerate.

And, I have seen it from wives. Years ago I had a seminary student working on an intern basis. He and his wife proceeded to take us out for lunch that day after church. She was a college graduate, a speech major — very competent. The minute we got in the car, she started on him. He was driving along — so proud and happy— he was taking the pastor out — he worked for the pastor — his boss. She turned to him and said, Bill, why can't you preach like Wayne preaches? Now this morning — look what he did— why can't you do that? I have been trying to tell you — this is the way to do it. And she went on and on. He gripped the wheel more tightly and his head got lower and lower. She finally quit when she had him beaten down. That is the way he lived. That is abuse.

Tenderhearted— tender — caring— upbuilding— uplifting. That is a Christian in a Christian family.

Let's get another word. *Security.* That is the very concept of marriage. When is a home Christian? It is when there is security in that marriage.

First of all, *physical security.* The little boy says, My daddy could whip anybody in all the world. He has a feeling that he is secure. Nobody is going to come in and hurt him. He is secure. And that is the basic idea in primitive marriage. The young lady said to me, My daddy said to me. I am so glad you are married to a good man who loves you and will take care of you. And I wanted that above everything else — someone who loves me and will take care of me.

Security is so important in life — we all need it. That is why the family is there, so you can say, We stand together — two of us against the world. He have security in each other and as the family grows, our family will stand. We will always be together.

There is an *emotional security* also that says, We will always be together, even when I may lose my job, or my beauty, or my health — I will always have some-body standing with me. That is emotional security. This works in a family where every member of that family says, They will never put me out — I will always have a place in the family.

192

An 81-year-old man lived with his son and daughter-in-law. He would sometimes have a bad night. One morning at breakfast the daughter-in-law said, How did you sleep, Dad? He said, I just feel sick, and he began to talk about his ailments, his hurts and his pains. She just blew up! I am getting sick and tired of this. This is not a happy way for breakfast — to hear you complaining about everything *that* is wrong. You have to get a positive attitude in life — you have to quit thinking about yourself. I don't want to hear anymore about this. He quietly ate a little bit of food and went upstairs and took a revolver out of the drawer and went to the garage and shot himself! Why? Because they said, We do not want to be bothered with you anymore.

Emotional security — I will always be accepted here. There is one place I can come. A boy can come back home saying, Well, I have one refuge. A girl can come back home saying, They still love me. I know I have done things wrong and they did not approve of what I did. But they will always accept me. They love me.

And there is moral security. The kind of trust and faith that you have in the moral integrity of the other one in marriage. The woman goes to work downtown and the husband does not worry. He has confidence in her — security in her morality — to know that she will not fall in love with the boss; or be preyed upon by the male predators who will try to seduce her in that office. She will be faithful. And she does not worry. She has the kind of moral security and trust in her husband that when he goes to Las Vegas to a convention, she does not worry about his getting off the track and doing something wrong out there.

Security — physical — psychological — moral. That makes a Christian family.

The last word is *faith*. You cannot have a Christian family without a person being a Christian in it. That is what a young man said when he came to see the pastor: Tell me how to be a Christian. I have just been in the home of the girl I am going to marry — And I saw a Christian family for the first time. I had never seen it except on television and I thought it was just a fable way of existence — but I saw it for real. They prayed at the table — they loved each other — they were so happy —they hugged and kissed each other as we came in to visit them. That is the kind of home I never had, and I want a Christian family. Tell me how to be a Christian. And that is the start. How can I be a Christian? That is where it starts for a Christian family.

If you are not a Christian, would you receive Christ as your Savior? If you are a Christian, maybe you need the family and fellowship of a church to help you grow as a Christian.